THE SENTENCES OF SEXTUS

Society of Biblical Literature

TEXTS AND TRANSLATIONS
EARLY CHRISTIAN LITERATURE SERIES

Robert L. Wilken and William R. Schoedel, Editors

Texts and Translations 22
Early Christian Literature Series Number 5

THE SENTENCES OF SEXTUS

by
Richard A. Edwards and Robert A. Wild, S. J.

THE SENTENCES OF SEXTUS

Edited and Translated by
Richard A. Edwards and
Robert A. Wild, S. J.

Scholars Press

Distributed by
Scholars Press
101 Salem St.
P.O. Box 2268
Chico, CA 95927

THE SENTENCES OF SEXTUS

Edited and Translated by
Richard A. Edwards and
Robert A. Wild, S. J.

Library of Congress Cataloging in Publication Data

Sextou gnōmai. English & Greek.
  The sentences of Sextus.

  (Early Christian literature series ; 5) (Texts and
translations ; no. 22)(ISSN 0145-322X)
    Translation of: Sextou gnōmai.
    English and Greek.
    Attributed to Sextus Pythagoreus ; also attributed to
Sixtus II—Encycl. Brit. and Cath. encycl.
    Bibliography: p.
    Includes index.
    1. Christian life—Early works to 1800. I. Edwards,
Richard Alan, 1934. II. Wild, Robert Anthony,
S. J., 1940. III. Sextus Pythagoreus. IV. Sixtus II. Pope, d. 258.
V. Title. VI. Series. VII. Series: Texts and translations. ;
no. 22.
BV4500.S49   248.4   81-13770
ISBN 0-89130-528-9   AACR2

Printed in the United States of America
1 2 3 4 5
Edwards Brothers, Inc.
Ann Arbor, Michigan 48106

INTRODUCTION

This collection of 451[1] sayings, comprised of a variety of specific forms, was probably compiled in Egypt[2] in the second century CE. It was well known among Christians particularly after the fourth century as a result of the Latin translation of Rufinus.[3] Such Gnomologia were quite popular in the Roman and Byzantine periods and the genre reached its greatest heights in the fifth century collection of Johannes Stobaeus. Although the author's identity as "Sextus" has not been finally demonstrated, it appears certain that the editor, whoever he was, was a Christian.[4] There are interesting, parallel, non-Christian collections which show some close similarity, thus indicating that it was possible to understand or interpret the type of materials found in the *Sentences* in a variety of ways. The character of the individual sayings (short, epigramatic, general) invites and actually demands that the hearer supply the interpretive context and framework.

The basic outlook of the present collection is best summarized by the phrase "mild asceticism." For example, the reader is advised to refrain from over-indulgence in food. In addition, despite the great danger of lust, the author assumes that some of his addressees are married. It is likewise assumed that they do indeed own property. There is no demand that possessions be rejected nor that the wise person retreat into the desert as a hermit. Rather the advice is: do not resist those who would take your possessions and always be willing to share them with those who ask. Perseverance or endurance is required because there are some things which cannot be changed. Although the recommended path is difficult, there is a quiet confidence that problems can be solved. The ideal person is the "sophos" and there is only a limited reference to "faith" and "faithfulness."[5]

Since people are weak and susceptible to evil, effort is demanded to maintain the standards of the wise. Only if the soul can control one's actions can it be one's guide. Those things which are valued include: wisdom, worthiness before God, things which are either similar to God or suitable for God, the things of the soul (in contrast to physical attributes or possessions), the sharing of both the understanding of God and one's possessions-- although each must be done with discretion.

To be wise is to be self-controlled, self-conscious and alert. All excesses are dangerous, including laughter. It is better to be temperate (chaste) than to cut off a limb. There is a definite sense of a positive correlation between body and soul, with the body being described as the seal or impression of the soul.

Up until quite recently, as is indicated by the appended bibliography, there has not been much scholarly consideration of the *Sentences* beyond the study of the text and versions. However, the discovery of the *Sentences* among the Nag Hammadi collection has reawakened interest, and this may yet lead to the investigation of important unanswered questions such as the place of the *Sentences* in the development of Egyptian Christianity. We hope that this text and translation will spur interest in the *Sentences of Sextus* as well as in the nature and extent of the use of wisdom traditions in early Christianity.

As far as we can determine, the only English translation was published by Conybeare in 1910 in a limited edition which is now very difficult to obtain. A problem with that version is the editor's choice of "King James" English for his translation.

With respect to the text in the twenty year period since H. Chadwick published his critical edition, an important new early witness was discovered among the Coptic codices at Nag Hammadi in Upper Egypt. This alone, if nothing else, made it necessary that we reconsider the state of the text. While the Greek text provided here remains substantially that of Chadwick, we have ventured

to suggest new readings and emendations for twenty-one
of the sayings. The accompanying apparatus indicates for
the most part only major variants. However, because the
Coptic fragments are here collated for the first time,
greater attention is given to their possible contribution
to the text.

Further work will be necessary in establishing a defi-
nitive text of the *Sentences* because, among other things,
numerous Latin manuscripts exist which have never been
collated and the Armenian version, although known for a
long time, has yet to be properly studied. So that the
reader may have a sufficient understanding of the various
witnesses for the text, we present this brief summation
of the evidence:

1. Two relatively late Greek manuscripts, Patmiensis
263 (tenth century) and Vaticanus Graecus 742 (fourteenth
century), are the sole witnesses for the *Sentences* in
its original language. Both manuscripts add further
sayings to the corpus, and the order of sayings in the
Patmos text differs quite significantly from that given
in the Vaticanus and in most of the versions.

2. About a quarter of the sayings, one hundred and
twenty-eight to be exact, are now attested in a Coptic
version. The manuscript in which the translation appears
dates from the fourth century and was a part of the Gnostic
library found at Nag Hammadi.[6] This version has proven
to be an important witness for the textual tradition. We
discovered forty-seven major variants attested by the
Coptic, although only eight of these proved to be peculiar
to it. Free translations are rare (cf. 325 and 387) and
notable redactional additions are found in only two
places (321 and 335). Interestingly, the majority of
the Coptic variants, thirty in all, agree with the chief
Syriac witness (sy^2); this may be an indication that the
Syriac text, despite its evident redactional additions,
is a more important source of information on the *Sentences* than has been previously thought. Of the Greek
manuscripts, the Coptic version agrees somewhat more often

with the Vatican (14 times) than with the Patmos text
(10 times); it was found *never* to agree with Patmos
against all other witnesses. Against the altered se-
quences of Patmos and sy^2, the Coptic confirms the ordering of the sayings found in Rufinus and in the Vatican
manuscript.[7]

    3. Separate Syriac translations of the *Sentences*
were made, apparently, in the fifth or sixth century;
these are preserved together in many manuscripts, the
oldest of which date to the mid-sixth century.[8] The chief
translation (sy^2 = X in the older editions) includes all
but sixty-three of the sayings found in Sextus 1-451.
There is also an epitome of 131 selected sayings (sy^1) and
a few additional sayings included as an appendix to the
overall collection contained in the manuscripts.[9] In
general, the tendency of the Syriac is to add redactional
explanations or applications to the original saying (gener-
ally kept intact) in order to connect it more explicitly
with Christian teaching or with the special concerns of
monastic communities. Because the core saying is usually
recoverable, the Syriac has definite value as a textual
witness.

    4. All of the numerous Latin manuscripts of the
Sentences go back to the translation made by Rufinus,
that quondam friend of St. Jerome, in the fourth century.[10]
This translation is important because it has served to
delimit the original length of the *Sentences*, i.e.,
those sayings encompassed within Sextus 1-451, and it func-
tions as an early and fairly conservative witness to the
original Greek text. Gildemeister, who made the original
collation of fourteen manuscripts, gave priority to two
early manuscripts, Salmasianus, Paris. 10318, 7th-8th
cen. AD (A) and Paris, lat. 2676, 9th cen. AD (Q).[11] His
hypothesis may still be correct since none of the manuscripts which have come to light since his time date
before the tenth century.

    5. Included in an Armenian translation of sayings
attributed to Evagrius Ponticus are about 130 sayings from

the original collection of the *Sentences*.[12] Although
Hermann has concluded that the Armenian actually trans-
lates the Greek text and not a Syriac version,[13] the rela-
tionship of this witness to the rest of the textual tradition remains poorly understood. According to Hermann,
this translation, despite occasional errors, misunder-
standings, and efforts to provide greater theological or
ascetical pointedness, follows the Greek original rather
closely.[14]

   With this overview of the textual tradition before
the reader, we are now able to say something further
about the form of the text adopted for this edition. In
the ordering and numbering of the sayings we have followed
the lead of our predecessors, A. Elter and H. Chadwick,
in using the Latin edition of Rufinus as a foundation.
That same order is also found for the most part in the
Vatican Greek manuscript although certain additions occur
there (i.e., those sayings with numbers ending in b, c,
d, e, etc.) and twenty-six sayings are omitted. The
Coptic provides further verification for this sequence
since it virtually always conforms to the order followed
by Rufinus and includes, at least where it is extant,
all the sayings omitted by the Vatican ms. In those
places where we have offered a text which differs from that
of Chadwick, it is usually because we believe that the
majority of witnesses (including in all but five cases
at least one and sometimes both of the Greek mss.) offer
an idiomatic and readable text not requiring the adoption
of a variant reading or an emendation. However, we have
utilized less well attested readings for sayings 13 and
442 because of probable New Testament influence upon the
majority text. In the case of the following sayings
(besides 442) the versions appear to provide a better
tradition: 298 (versions agree against Π; Y conflates),
322 (three separate versions agree against Π and Y), and
394 (the Coptic offers a solution to a confused textual
tradition). We have particularly questioned particles
and conjunctions which link a saying with its immediate

6

predecessor (Sayings 10, 230a, 347, and 354) unless such words are very strongly attested (e.g., Saying 374).

Edwards and Wild worked together to produce the final translation. Edwards began a study of the *Sentences* while a member of Wayne Meeks's 1977 N.E.H. Summer Seminar and wishes to acknowledge the help and support of both Professor Meeks and the Endowment. Wild has studied the Coptic manuscript and did the major portion of the work on the textual notes.

We also wish to thank the editors of the series, Robert Wilken and William Schoedel, and the former editor, Birger Pearson, for their advice and encouragement.

Two graduate assistants, Guy Carter and Joyce Little, have also assisted at various points along the way. And a special thanks to Camille Slowinski for her careful typing and to Mary Lou Doyle for preparing the final copy.

NOTES

[1] The number of sayings in the collection and their order is not consistent in the texts and versions. Cf. Chadwick, pp. 1-8.

[2] Egypt is most often suggested because the earliest references to Sextus are found in Origen.

[3] On the Latin translation, cf. especially Chadwick, pp. 9-63.

[4] Chadwick, pp. 138-162.

[5] πιστεύω appears 3 times, πίστις 8 times, and πιστός 30 times.

[6] Codex 12, ff. 15-16 and 27-34. See *The Facsimile Edition of the Nag Hammadi Codices: Codices XI, XII and XIII* (ed. James M. Robinson *et al.*; Leiden, 1973) 85-94. Translation by Frederik Wisse, *The Nag Hammadi Library in English* (New York, 1977) 454-59.

[7] The Coptic, however, omits 162a and places 333 after 334 and 355 after 357.

[8] For a listing of these manuscripts see A. Baumstark, *Geschichte der syrischen Literatur* (Bonn, 1922), 170, n. 6. The only edition of these is still that of Paul de Lagarde (*Analecta syriaca* [Leipzig, 1858] 2-31).

[9] For translations of the Syriac see J. Gildemeister [bibliography] and V. Ryssel [bibliography].

[10] Bogaert (*Revue Benedictine* 82 [1972] 32-35) records a total of some fifty manuscripts, over three times as many as those listed by Chadwick (*Sentences*, pp. 4-5). These have not yet been collated.

[11] Gildemeister, pp. xxv-xxx. Manuscript Q includes only sentences 1-84.

[12] The sole available edition is that of Sarkisian (Venice, 1907). For an Eng. trans. see Conybeare, pp. 131-38.

[13] Hermann, *Zeitschrift für Kirchengeschichte* 57 (1938) 220.

[14] Ibid., 225-26.

SELECT BIBLIOGRAPHY

I. Texts and Versions

Chadwick, Henry, *The Sentences of Sextus* (Texts and Studies 5; Cambridge, Eng., 1959). [Currently available as a Kraus reprint.]

Conybeare, F. C., *The Ring of Pope Xystus* (London, 1910).

Elter, Anton, *Gnomica I: Sexti Pythagorici, Clitarchi, Evagrii Pontici sententiae* (Leipzig, 1892).

The Facsimile Edition of the Nag Hammadi Codices: Codices XI, XII and XIII (ed. J. M. Robinson *et al.*: Leiden, 1973) xiii-xv and 85-94.

Gildemeister, Johann, *Sexti Sententiarum recensiones latinam, graecam, syriacas* (Bonn, 1873).

Hermann, T., "Die armenische Überlieferung der Sextussentenzen," *Zeitschrift für Kirchengeschichte* 57 (1938) 217-26.

Kroll, J., "Die Sprüche des Sextus," *Neutestamentliche Apokryphen* (ed. E. Hennecke; 2nd ed. [only], Tübingen, 1924) 625-43.

Lagarde, Paul de, *Analecta syriaca* (Leipzig, 1858).

Ryssel, V., "Die syrische Übersetzung der Sextussentenzen," *Zeitschrift für wissenschaftliche Theologie* 38 (1895) 617-30; 39 (1896) 568-624; 40 (1897) 131-48.

II. Studies (for other older literature see Chadwick, *Sentences*, 182-83)

Bogaert, P.-M., "La préface de Rufin aux Sentences de Sexte et a une oeuvre inconnue," *Revue bénédictine* 82 (1972) 24-46.

Broek, R. van den, "Niet-gnostisch Christendom in Alexandrië voor Clemens en Origines," *Nederlands Theologisch Tijdschrift* 33 (1979) 287-99.

Chadwick, Henry, "The Sentences of Sextus and of the Pythagoreans," *Journal of Theological Studies* 11 (1960) 349.

9

Delling, Gerhard, "Zur Hellenisierung des Christen-
    tums in den 'Sprüchen des Sextus'," *Studien
    zum Neuen Testament und zur Patristik.
    Festschrift für Erich Klostermann* (Texte und
    Untersuchungen 77; Berlin, 1961) 208-41.

Gwynn, J., "Xystus," *Dictionary of Christian
    Biography* 4 (1887) 1198-1205.

Harnack, Adolf von, "Sextus [Xystus] Sprüche,"
    *Geschichte der altchristlichen Litteratur bis
    Eusebius* (ed. A. von Harnack: vol. 2, pt. 2;
    Leipzig, 1904) 190-92.

Kroll, W., "Sextus[5]", *Realencyclopädie der class-
    ischen Wissenschaft* 2.2.2 (Stuttgart, 1923)
    2061-64.

Pezzella, S. "Le rapport des Sentences de Sextius et
    de la lettre a Marcella de Porphyre," *La nouvelle
    Clio* 10-12 (1958-62) 252-53.

Silvestre, Hubert, "Trois nouveaux témoins latins
    des *Sentences* de Sextus," *Scriptorium* 17 (1963)
    128-29.

Vogüé, A. de, "'Ne juger de rien par soi-meme': Deux
    emprunts de la Règle colombanienne aux Sentences
    de Sextus et à S. Jérôme," *Revue d'histoire de
    la spiritualité* 49 (1973) 129-34.

Wilken, Robert L., "Wisdom and Philosophy in Early
    Christianity," *Aspects of Wisdom in Judaism and
    Early Christianity* (ed. Robert L. Wilken;
    Notre Dame, IN, 1975), 143-68.

Wisse, Frederik, "Die Sextus-Sprüche und das Problem
    der gnostischen Ethik," *Zum Hellenismus in den
    Schriften von Nag Hammadi* (ed. A. Böhlig and
    F. Wisse; Göttinger Orientforschungen 6.2;
    Wiesbaden, 1975) 55-86.

Zeller, E., *Die Philosophie der Griechen*, vol. 3,
    pt. 1 (4th ed.; Leipzig, 1909) 701-4.

SCRIPTURE INDEX

Sigla:

Π	Patmiensis 263 saec. X
Y	Vaticanus Graecus saec. XIV
lat	individual Latin mss. (e.g., A, Q, etc.-- see Chadwick, pp. 4-5)
latt	all mss. presently collated
sy^1	Syriac epitome (ed. Lagarde, 2.1-10.21)
sy^2	more complete Syriac translation (ed. Lagarde, 10.22-25.11)
syy	both Syriac traditions
copt	Coptic translation (157-180, 307-97)
Ch.	Chadwick, *Sentences*
Elt.	Elter
Gild.	Gildemeister
m	many witnesses
pl	most witnesses
pm	the majority of remaining witnesses
rell	all witnesses except those enumerated with the full stop

13

TEXT AND TRANSLATION

ΣΕΞΤΟΥ ΓΝΩΜΑΙ

1   Πιστὸς ἄνθρωπος ἐκλεκτός ἐστιν ἄνθρωπος.

2   ἐκλεκτὸς ἄνθρωπος ἄνθρωπός ἐστι θεοῦ.

3   θεοῦ ἄνθρωπος ὁ ἄξιος θεοῦ.

4   θεοῦ ἄξιος ὁ μηδὲν ἀνάξιον θεοῦ πράττων.

5   ἐπιτηδεύων οὖν πιστὸς εἶναι μηδὲν ἀνάξιον θεοῦ πράξῃς.

6   ὀλιγόπιστος ἐν πίστει ἄπιστος.

7a   πιστὸς ἐν δοκιμῇ πίστεως θεὸς ἐν ἀνθρώπου σώματι ζῶντι.

7b   ἄπιστος ἐν πίστει νεκρὸς ἄνθρωπος ἐν σώματι ζῶντι.

8   πιστὸς ἀληθείᾳ ὁ ἀναμάρτητος.

9   μέχρι καὶ τῶν ἐλαχίστων ἀκριβῶς βίου.

10   οὐ μικρὸν ἐν βίῳ τὸ παρὰ μικρόν.

11   πᾶν ἁμάρτημα ἀσέβημα ἡγοῦ.

12   οὐκ ὀφθαλμὸς οὐδὲ χεὶρ ἁμαρτάνει οὐδέ τι τῶν ὁμοίων,
      ἀλλ' ὁ κακῶς χρώμενος χειρὶ καὶ ὀφθαλμῷ.

13   πᾶν μέρος τοῦ σώματος ἀναπεῖθόν σε μὴ σωφρονεῖν
      ῥῖψον· ἄμεινον γὰρ χωρὶς τοῦ μέρους ζῆν σωφρόνως
      ἢ μετὰ τοῦ μέρους ὀλεθρίως.

14   ἀθανάτους σοι νόμιζε παρὰ τῇ κρίσει καὶ τὰς τιμὰς
      ἔσεσθαι καὶ τὰς τιμωρίας.

15   ὁπόσα τοῦ κόσμου ἔχεις, κἂν ἀφέληταί σού τις,
      μὴ ἀγανάκτει.

Title] om. Y (Idem titulus inseritur post 190 et 276 Π).
4   θεοῦ . . . πράττων] Π lat^Q Elt. Ch.: ἀνάξιος ὁ
μηδὲν ἄξιον θεοῦ πράττων Y: . . . qui dignum Deo agit
lat^A: . . . qui nihil indigne agit rell. lat.
7a Om. Π latt. Cf. Seneca, Ep. 31.11.
9   Cf. Lk. 16.10.
10 οὐ] Π latt.: οὐ γὰρ Y (sy^2?) Elt. Ch.
11 = 297b.
12 ἀλλ' . . . . ὀφθαλμῷ] Π: ἀλλὰ τὸ κακῶς ὁρώμενον ἐν
χειρὶ καὶ ὀφθαλμῷ Y: . . . τὸ κακῶς δρώμενον . . . .sy^2:
. . . . τὸ κακῶς χρώμενον χειρὶ καὶ ὀφθαλμῷ pl. lat.
13 μέρος (ubique) Orig. (Comm. in Matt. 15.3): μέλος Π
Y Elt. Ch. (cf. Mt. 5.29-30) / τοῦ σώματος] om. Orig.
m. lat / σωφρόνως] Y Orig. sy^2: om. Π latt. Cf.
also Mt. 18.8-9 / Mk. 9.43-47.

THE SENTENCES OF SEXTUS

1   A faithful man is an elect man.

2   An elect man is a man of God.

3   A man of God is worthy of God.

4   One worthy of God does nothing unworthy of God.

5   Therefore if you wish to be faithful, do nothing unworthy of God.

6   Regarding faith, a man of little faith is without faith.

7a In a trial of faith, a faithful person is a god in a living human body.

7b Regarding faith, a faithless person is a dead man in a living body.

8   A sinless person is truly faithful.

9   Even in regard to the smallest matters, live scrupulously.

10 In human life even the smallest thing is not trivial.

11 Consider every sin a sacrilege.

12 It is neither eye nor hand nor any such thing that sins, but he who misuses hand and eye.

13 Cast away any part of the body which leads you to intemperance; for it is better to live temperately without it than to perish whole.

14 Consider that at the judgment both your rewards and your punishments will be eternal.

15 Even if someone takes away your worldly possessions, do not be vexed.

18

16 σεαυτὸν ἐπιλήψιμον μὴ πάρεχε τῷ κόσμῳ.

17 χωρὶς τῆς ἐλευθερίας πάντα ἀφαιρουμένῳ σε τῷ
    πέλας ὕπεικε.

18 σοφὸς ἀκτήμων ὅμοιος θεῷ.

19 τοῖς κοσμικοῖς πράγμασιν εἰς αὐτὰ τὰ ἀναγκαῖα χρῶ.

20 τὰ μὲν τοῦ κόσμου τῷ κόσμῳ, τὰ δὲ τοῦ θεοῦ τῷ θεῷ
    ἀκριβῶς ἀποδίδου.

21 τὴν ψυχήν σου νόμιζε παραθήκην ἔχειν παρὰ θεοῦ.

22 ὅτε λέγεις περὶ θεοῦ, κρίνῃ ὑπὸ θεοῦ.

23 ἄριστον ἡγοῦ καθαρμὸν τὸ μηδένα ἀδικεῖν.

24 ψυχὴ καθαίρεται λόγῳ θεοῦ ὑπὸ σοφοῦ.

25 ἀναίσθητον οὐσίαν μὴ πεισθῇς εἶναί ποτε θεοῦ.

26 ὁ θεὸς καθὸ νοῦς ἐστιν αὐτοκίνητος, κατ᾽ αὐτὸ τοῦτο
    καὶ ὑφέστηκεν.

27 θεοῦ μέγεθος οὐκ ἂν ἐξεύροις πτεροῖς πετόμενος.

28 θεοῦ ὄνομα μὴ ζήτει, οὐ γὰρ εὑρήσεις·πᾶν τὸ
    ὀνομαζόμενον ὀνομάζεται ὑπὸ τοῦ κρείττονος, ἵνα
    τὸ μὲν καλῇ, τὸ δὲ ὑπακούῃ· τίς οὖν ὁ ὀνομάσας
    θεόν; θεὸς οὐκ ὄνομα θεοῦ, ἀλλὰ δόξα περὶ θεοῦ.

29 μηθὲν οὖν ἐν θεῷ ὃ μὴ ἔστι ζήτει.

30 θεὸς αὐγὴ σοφὴ τοῦ ἐναντίου ἀνεπίδεκτος.

31 ὁ θεὸς ὅσα ἐποίησεν, ὑπὲρ ἀνθρώπων αὐτὰ ἐποίησεν.

32 ἄγγελος ὑπηρέτης θεοῦ πρὸς ἄνθρωπον, οὐ γὰρ δὴ πρὸς
    οὐδένα ἄλλον· τιμιώτερον οὖν ἄνθρωπος ἀγγέλου
    παρὰ θεῷ.

---

20 Cf. Mt. 22.21 / Mk. 12.17 / Lk. 20.25.
28 Referred to by Maximus Conf., *Schol. in Dion. Areop.*
    (*PG* 4.429B). John of Damascus cites the saying
    but attributes it to Babylas of Antioch (*PG* 96.533A).
32 οὐδένα ἄλλον] Υ: οὐδέν Π lat[AQ]: οὐδὲν ἄλλο sy[2]
    (om. οὐ . . . ἄλλον rell. lat).

16   Do not offer the world a chance to criticize you.

17   Let your neighbor take away everything except your
     freedom.

18   A sage without property is like God.

19   Use worldly things only when necessary.

20   Take care to render to the world the things of the
     world and to God the things of God.

21   Consider that your soul is a trust from God.

22   When you speak about God, you are judged by God.

23   Recognize that the best purification is to harm
     no one.

24   A soul is purified by a word of God from a sage.

25   Do not be persuaded that the being of God is ever
     insensible.

26   God is self-moving because He is mind; for this
     reason He is also subsistent.

27   Though you fly with wings you cannot discover the
     greatness of God.

28   Do not seek God's name, for you will not find it.
     Everything that has a name is named by someone more
     powerful, that the one might call and the other obey.
     Who then has named God? 'God' is not the name of God
     but a conception about God.

29   Therefore do not seek anything in God which is not
     possible.

30   God is the wise light which has no room for its
     opposite.

31   Whatever God has done, He has done for the sake of
     humanity.

32   An angel is a minister of God to man, for he
     ministers to no one else. Therefore, in God's sight,
     a man is of more value than an angel.

20

33 τὸ μὲν πρῶτον εὐεργετοῦν ὁ θεός, τὸ δὲ δεύτερον
εὐεργετούμενον ἄνθρωπος.

34 βίου τοιγαροῦν ὡς ὢν μετὰ θεόν.

35 ἐκλεκτὸς ὢν ἔχεις τι ἐν τῇ συστάσει σου ὁποῖον θεός·
χρῶ οὖν τῇ συστάσει σου ὡς ἱερῷ θεοῦ.

36 ἐξουσίαν πιστῷ ὁ θεὸς δίδωσι τὴν κατὰ θεόν· καθαρὰν
οὖν δίδωσι καὶ ἀναμάρτητον.

37 αἰδείσθω σου τὸν βίον ὁ κόσμος.

38 μηδενὶ σεαυτὸν ἐπιλήψιμον δίδου.

39 κακῶς ζῶντα μετὰ τὴν ἀπαλλαγὴν τοῦ σώματος εὐθύνει
κακὸς δαίμων μέχρις οὗ καὶ τὸν ἔσχατον κοδράντην
ἀπολάβῃ.

40 μακάριος ἀνήρ, οὗ τῆς ψυχῆς οὐδεὶς ἐπιλήψεται
εἰς θεὸν πορευομένης.

41 ὃ ἂν τιμήσῃς ὑπὲρ πάντα, ἐκεῖνό σου κυριεύσει.

42 τίμα τὸ ἄριστον, ἵνα καὶ ἄρχῃ ὑπὸ τοῦ ἀρίστου.

43 ἀρχόμενος ὑπὸ τοῦ ἀρίστου αὐτὸς ἄρξεις ὧν ἂν
προαιρῇ.

44 τιμὴ μεγίστη θεῷ θεοῦ γνῶσις καὶ ὁμοίωμα.

45 ὅμοιον μὲν οὐδὲν θεῷ, προσφιλέστατον δὲ τὸ εἰς
δύναμιν ἐξομοιούμενον.

46a ἱερὸν ἅγιον θεοῦ διάνοια εὐσεβοῦς.

46b ἄριστον θυσιαστήριον θεῷ καρδία καθαρὰ καὶ ἀναμάρτητος.

47 θυσία θεῷ μόνη καὶ προσηνὴς ἡ ἀνθρώποις εὐεργεσία
διὰ θεόν.

---

34 μετὰ θεόν] Y: μετὰ θεὸν ὁ δεύτερος pl. lat sy^2:
μετὰ θεοῦ Π.
36 Cited by Pelagius (Augustine, *De nat. et grat.* 64.77).
39 εὐθύνει] Π Elt. Ch.: εὐθυνεῖ latt; εὐθύνοι κακῶς Y.
Cf. Mt. 5.26.
45 Cf. Plato, *Theat.* 176B.
46a Cited by Pelagius (Augustine, *De nat. et grat.* 64.77).
46b Cited by Pelagius (Ibid.).

33 First of all there is God the benefactor, secondly
man the beneficiary.

34 Live therefore as one who is next in rank after God.

35 Because you are elect, you have within yourself
something God-like. Therefore treat yourself as a
temple of God.

36 God gives divine power to a faithful person; that is,
He gives pure and sinless power.

37 Let the world respect your way of life.

38 Do not give anyone a reason to criticize you.

39 After he is released from his body, the evil person
will be called to account by an evil demon until the
last penny is paid up.

40 Blessed is the man whose soul no one attacks as it
journeys toward God.

41 Whatever you honor most will rule you.

42 Honor what is best that you may be governed by what
is best.

43 If you are governed by what is best, you yourself
will govern whatever you choose.

44 The knowledge and imitation of God is the best way
to honor Him.

45 Nothing is like God, but whatever imitates Him as
far as possible is most pleasing to Him.

46a The mind of a pious man is a holy temple of God.

46b A pure and sinless heart is the finest altar dedicated
to God.

47 The only suitable offering to God is to do good
deeds for men because of God.

48 ἄνθρωπος κεχαρισμένα θεῷ πράττει ὁ ζῶν εἰς
   δύναμιν κατὰ θεόν.
49 ὁ μὲν θεὸς οὐδενὸς δεῖται, ὁ δὲ πιστὸς μόνου θεοῦ.
50 ζηλοῖ τὸν οὐδενὸς δεόμενον ὁ τῶν ὀλίγων ἀναγκαίως
   δεόμενος.
51 ἄσκει μέγας μὲν εἶναι παρὰ θεῷ, παρὰ δὲ ἀνθρώποις
   ἀνεπίφθονος.
52 χρηστὸς ὢν εἰς τοὺς δεομένους μέγας ἂν εἴης
   παρὰ θεῷ.
53 ἀνδρὸς σοφοῦ ζῶντος μὲν ὀλίγος ὁ λόγος παρὰ ἀνθρώποις,
   τελευτήσαντος δὲ τὸ κλέος ᾄδεται.
54 τὸν χρόνον ὃν ἂν μὴ νοήσῃς τὸν θεόν, τοῦτον
   νόμιζέ σοι ἀπολωλέναι.
55 τὸ μὲν σῶμά σου μόνον ἐπιδημείτω τῇ γῇ, ἡ δὲ
   ψυχὴ ἀεὶ ἔστω παρὰ θεῷ.
56 νόει τὰ καλά, ἵνα καὶ πράττῃς τὰ καλά.
57a ἔννοια ἀνθρώπου θεὸν οὐ λανθάνει.
57b ἔστω σου ἡ διάνοια καθαρὰ κακοῦ παντός.
58 ἄξιος ἔσο τοῦ ἀξιώσαντός σε εἰπεῖν υἱὸν καὶ
   πρᾶττε πάντα ὡς υἱὸς θεοῦ.
59 θεὸν πατέρα καλῶν ἐν οἷς πράττεις τούτου μέμνησο.
60 ἁγνὸς ἀνὴρ καὶ ἀναμάρτητος ἐξουσίαν ἔχει παρὰ θεῷ
   ὡς υἱὸς θεοῦ.

---

49 πιστός] Y latt sy¹: πιστὸς καὶ σοφὸς Π (Pagan
   versions of this saying [Clitarchus 4; Pyth. 39;
   Porphyry, *Ad. Marc.* 11] read σοφός).
57a θεὸν οὐ] Π latt: om. Y.
58 ἔσο] latt. Elt. Ch.: ἔσω Y: ἔση Π / υἱον . . .
   πρᾶττε] Y latt: υἱὸν θεοῦ. Πρᾶττε οὖν Π.
59 = 222. Om Y.
60 Om. Y / ἔχει] lat^G Elt. Ch.: ἔχῃ Π: *accipiet*
   latΩ: *accepit* rell. lat Aug. Cited by Pelagius
   (Augustine, *De nat. et grat.* 64.77).

48 A person pleases God when he lives as far as possible in accordance with God.
49 God needs no one; the faithful man needs only God.
50 The person who requires little for his needs emulates Him who needs nothing.
51 Endeavor to be great in God's sight yet without reproach among men.
52 If you are good to the needy, you will be great in God's sight.
53 While a wise man is alive his fame among men is small, but after his death men sing his praises.
54 Consider as lost the time you do not spend thinking about God.
55 Let your body alone be at home on earth; let your soul be always with God.
56 Think about good things so that you may also do good things.
57a A person's thoughts do not escape God.
57b Let your mind be free of all evil.
58 Be worthy of the One who deems you worthy to be called a son and act always as a son of God.
59 You call God "Father": remember this in your actions.
60 A chaste and sinless man has power in God's sight as a son of God.

24

61 ἀγαθὴ διάνοια χῶρος θεοῦ.

62 κακὴ διάνοια χῶρός ἐστιν κακῶν.

63 τὸν ἀδικοῦντα τοῦ ἀδικεῖν ἀπαλλάττων κολάζοις
    ἂν κατὰ θεόν.

64 ἄσκει μὴ τὸ δοκεῖν ἀλλὰ τὸ εἶναι δίκαιος· τὸ δοκεῖν
    γὰρ ἕκαστον τοῦ εἶναι ἀφαιρεῖται.

65 τίμα τὸ δίκαιον δι' αὐτό.

66 οὐκ ἂν λάθοις θεὸν πράττων ἄδικα, οὐδὲ γὰρ
    διανοούμενος.

67 σώφρων ἀνὴρ ἁγνὸς παρὰ τῷ θεῷ.

68 ἀκολασίαν φεῦγε.

69 εὐλογιστίαν ἄσκει.

70 κράτει τῶν ἡδονῶν.

71a νίκα τὸ σῶμα ἐν παντί.

71b ἐκ φιληδονίας ἀκολασίαν οὐκ ἐκφεύξῃ.

72 φιληδόνου ὁ θεὸς οὐκ ἀκούει.

73 τρυφῆς πέρας ὄλεθρος.

74 ὁ λόγος σου τῶν πράξεων προηγείσθω.

75a δεινότατόν ἐστιν πάθεσι δουλεύειν.

75b ὅσα πάθη ψυχῆς, τοσοῦτοι δεσπόται.

76 φιλοχρηματία φιλοσωματίας ἔλεγχος.

77 κτῶ τὰ τῆς ψυχῆς ὡς βέβαια.

78 ἀποτάττου τοῖς τοῦ σώματος, ἐφ' ὅσον δυνατὸς εἶ.

79 μόνον οἰκεῖον ἡγοῦ τὸ ἀγαθόν.

80 ὁποῖος θέλεις εὐχόμενος εἶναι, ἀεὶ ἔσο.

81 ὅταν τὰ κάλλιστα τῶν κτημάτων εὐλόγως εἰς βόρβορον
    ῥίψῃς, τότε καθαρὸς ὢν αἰτοῦ τι παρὰ τοῦ θεοῦ.

---

66 Included in an apotheom attributed to Thales
    (Diogenes Laertius 1.36).
67 σώφρων] Π Υ: σοφός latt / ἁγνὸς] Υ latt:₁ ἀγαθὸς Π.
74 πράξεων] Π latt Elt.: τῆς πράξεως σου sy¹:
    ὁρμῶν σου Υ Ch. (secundum Porphyry, *Ad. Marc.* 34).
    Cf. Sir. 37.16.

61 A good mind is the abode of God.

62 An evil mind is the abode of evil things.

63 If you release an unrighteous person from his wrong-doing, you punish him as God would.

64 Endeavor not to appear righteous but to be righteous, for appearance always usurps true being.

65 Honor righteousness for its own sake.

66 Even less than you can hide your thoughts can you hide your unjust acts from God.

67 The temperate man is pure in God's sight.

68 Flee licentiousness.

69 Exercise prudence.

70 Master pleasures.

71a Conquer the body in every way.

71b If you love pleasure, you will not escape licentious-ness.

72 God does not listen to one who loves pleasure.

73 Luxurious living results in ruin.

74 Let reason guide your actions.

75a It is terrible to be a slave to passion.

75b The soul has as many masters as it has passions.

76 Love of money demonstrates love of body.

77 Acquire the things of the soul because they are secure.

78 Put aside the things of the body as much as you can.

79 Consider only the good as your own.

80 Whatever sort of person you desire to be when pray-ing, be such always.

81 When you purposely throw your best possessions in the mud, then, being pure, ask for something from God.

26

82a   ὁποῖος θέλεις εἶναι παρὰ θεῷ, ἤδη ἔσο.

82b   τῶν τοῦ κόσμου μεταδιδοὺς καταφρόνει.

82c   μέμνησο ὧν μετὰ θεόν.

82d   ψυχὴ ἀνθρώπου θεοσεβοῦς θεὸς ἐν σώματι.

82e   μιαίνει τὸν θεὸν ὁ κακῶς νοῶν τὸν θεόν.

83   γλῶσσα βλάσφημος διανοίας ἔλεγχος κακῆς.

84   γλῶσσαν εὔφημον κέκτησο, μάλιστα δὲ περὶ θεοῦ.

85   κακῶς μὲν ποιῆσαι θεὸν δυνατὸς οὐδείς, ἀσεβέστατος
      δὲ ὁ βλασφημῶν· δυνατὸς γὰρ ὢν κἂν ἐποίησεν.

86a   κρηπὶς εὐσεβείας ἐγκράτεια.

86b   τέλος εὐσεβείας φιλία πρὸς θεόν.

87   χρῶ τῷ εὐσεβεῖ ὡς σαυτῷ.

88   εὔχου σοι γενέσθαι μὴ ἃ βούλει, ἀλλ᾽ ἃ δεῖ καὶ
      συμφέρει.

89   ὡς θέλεις χρήσασθαί σοι τοὺς πέλας, καὶ σὺ χρῶ
      αὐτοῖς.

90   ἃ ψέγεις, μηδὲ ποίει.

91a   μηδείς σε πειθέτω ποιεῖν τι παρὰ τὸ βέλτιον.

91b   ἃ δέδοταί σοι, κἂν ἀφέληταί σού τις, μὴ ἀγανάκτει.

92   ἃ δίδωσιν ὁ θεός, οὐδεὶς ἀφαιρεῖται.

93   σκέπτου πρὸ τοῦ πράττειν ἃ πράττεις ἵνα μὴ δὶς
      ποιῇς ἃ μὴ δεῖ.

82c   θεόν] Π latt: Θεοῦ Y.
83   Attributed to Plutarch (Maximus, *PG*. 91.784D).
86   Cf. Xenophon, *Mem*. 1.5.4 (ἀρετῆς); Philo, *De som*.
      1.124 (βίου).
89   = 210b. Cf. Mt. 7.12 / Lk. 6.31. For a Hellenistic
      version see Isocrates, *Nic*. 61.
91a   ποιεῖν] Π lat^S sy2: *petere* rell. lat: om. Y.
92   = 404 (ὅσα).
93   πράττειν . . . δεῖ] Π Y (sy²?): πράττειν καὶ ἃ
      πράττεις ἐξέταζε, ἵνα μηδὲν ποιῇς ὃ μὴ δεῖ coni. Elt
      (secundum Clitarchus 16) latt; Ch.

82a Whatever sort of person you desire to be in God's
     sight, be such now.
82b Despise worldly things by sharing them.
82c Remember that you are next in rank after God.
82d The soul of a pious man is a god in a body.
82e Whoever thinks evil of God defiles God.
83   A blasphemous tongue is proof of an evil mind.
84   Let your tongue speak good, especially about God.
85   No one can inflict evil upon God; but the blasphemer
     is the most impious, for, if he could, he would do
     God harm.
86a Self-control is the foundation of piety.
86b The goal of piety is friendship with God.
87   Treat a pious person as yourself.
88   Pray that you will be given not what you wish but
     what is necessary and useful.
89   As you expect your neighbors to treat you, so treat
     them.
90   Whatever you criticize, do not do.
91a Let no one persuade you to do what is not best.
91b Even if someone takes away what has been given
     to you, do not be vexed.
92   No one takes away what God gives.
93   Think carefully before undertaking any action
     lest you repeat an error.

28

94   ὃ πράττων οὐκ ἂν θέλοις εἰδέναι τὸν θεόν, τοῦτο
     μὴ πράξῃς.
95a πρὸ παντὸς οὗ πράττεις νόει τὸν θεόν.
95b φῶς σου τῶν πράξεων προηγείσθω.
96   μεγίστη ἀσέβεια εἰς θεὸν ἀνθρώπου κάκωσις.
97   ψυχὴ φωτίζεται ἐννοίᾳ θεοῦ.
98   αὐτάρκειαν ἄσκει.
99   τῶν ἀτόπων μὴ ὀρέγου.
100 τῶν καλῶν ἐκπόνει τὰ αἴτια.
101 τὰ τοῦ σώματος μὴ ἀγάπα.
102 ἀκάθαρτον ἄνθρωπον ποιεῖ πρᾶξις αἰσχρά.
103 καθαίρει ψυχὴν ἀνοήτου δόξης ἔλεγχος.

104 ὁ θεὸς ἀνθρώπων καλῶν πράξεων ἡγεμών ἐστιν.
105 μηδένα ἐχθρὸν ἡγοῦ.
106a άγάπα τὸ ὁμόφυλον.
106b ἀγάπα τὸν θεὸν καὶ πρὸ τῆς ψυχῆς σου.
107 οὐ χαλεπὸν ἁμαρτωλοὺς ἐπὶ τὸ αὐτὸ γενέσθαι μὴ
     ἁμαρτάνοντας.
108a τροφαὶ πολλαὶ ἁγνείαν ἐμποδίζουσιν.
108b ἀκρασία σιτίων ἀκάθαρτον ποιεῖ.
109 ἐμψύχων ἁπάντων χρῆσις μὲν ἀδιάφορον, ἀποχὴ δὲ
     λογικώτερον.
110 οὐ τὰ εἰσιόντα διὰ τοῦ στόματος σιτία καὶ ποτὰ
     μιαίνει τὸν ἄνθρωπον, ἀλλὰ τὰ ἀπὸ κακοῦ ἤθους
     ἐξιόντα.
111 ὃ ἂν ⟨ἡδονῇ⟩ ἡττώμενος σιτίον προσφέρῃ μιαίνει σε.
112 πλήθει ἀρέσκειν μὴ ἐπιτήδευε.

95b Ante φῶς add. ὅπως γνῶς ἀνθρώπων κάκωσιν Υ.
98   = 334. Om. Π.
99   ἀτόπων] Π sy² Ch.:   ἁπάντων Υ latt Elt.
104 Om. Υ.
106a Mt. 22.37, 39 / Mk. 12.30-31 / Lk. 10.27.
106b Mt. 22.37, 39 and parr.
107 Om. Π / οὐ] Υ sy² Ch.: om. latt Elt.
109 Cited by Origen (C. Cels. 8.30).
110 μιαίνει] Υ: κοινοῖ Π (Mt. 15.11).   Cf. Mt. 15.11.
111 ⟨ἡδονῇ⟩] coni. Ch. (cf. latt sy²):   om. Π Υ.

94   Whatever actions you do not want God to know, do
     not do.
95a Before you do anything, think about God.
95b Let your light guide your deeds.
96   The greatest impiety toward God is the mistreatment
     of a human being.
97   A soul is enlightened by reflection upon God.
98   Practice self-sufficiency.
99   Do not long for what is unnatural.
100 Search out the causes of good things.
101 Do not love what belongs to the body.
102 Shameful acts make a man impure.
103 The refutation of foolish opinion cleanses the soul.
104 God guides the good deeds of men.
105 Consider no one to be an enemy.
106a Love whatever is akin to you.
106b Love God even more than your own soul.
107 It is not difficult for sinners to associate with
     one another if they do not sin.
108a Too much food hinders purity.
108b Excessive eating leads to impurity.
109 The eating of any animal is a morally indifferent
     act, but it is more in accord with reason to abstain.
110 A person is not defiled by the food and drink which
     he consumes but by those acts which result from an
     evil character.
111 Whatever food you eat under the influence of pleasure
     defiles you.
112 Do not try to please the crowd.

30

113 παντὸς οὗ καλῶς πράττεις αἴτιον ἡγοῦ τὸν θεόν.
114 κακῶν θεὸς ἀναίτιος.
115 μὴ πλέον κτῶ ὧν τὸ σῶμα ἐπιζητεῖ.
116 ψυχὴν χρυσὸς οὐ ῥύεται κακῶν.
117 οὐ γέγονας ἐντρυφήσων τῇ τοῦ θεοῦ παρασκευῇ.
118 κτῶ ἃ μηδείς σου ἀφαιρεῖται.
119 φέρε τὰ ἀναγκαῖα ὡς ἀναγκαῖα.
120 μεγαλοψυχίαν ἄσκει.
121a ὧν καταφρονῶν ἐπαινῇ εὐλόγως, τούτων μὴ περιέχου.
121b ἐφ' οἷς εὐλόγως μεγαλοφρονεῖς, ταῦτα κέκτησο.
122 εὔχου τῷ θεῷ τὰ ἄξια τοῦ θεοῦ.
123 τὸν ἐν σοὶ λόγον τοῦ βίου σου νόμον ποίει.
124 αἰτοῦ παρὰ θεοῦ ἃ μὴ λάβοις ἂν παρὰ ἀνθρώπου.
125 ὧν ἡγεμόνες οἱ πόνοι, ταῦτά σοι εὔχου γενέσθαι
      μετὰ τοὺς πόνους.
126 εὐχὴ ῥᾳθύμου μάταιος λόγος.
127 ὧν τοῦ σώματος ἀπαλλαγεὶς οὐ δεήσῃ, καταφρόνει.
128 ὃ κτησάμενος οὐ καθέξεις, μὴ αἰτοῦ παρὰ θεοῦ.
129 ἔθιζε τὴν ψυχήν σου μετὰ θεὸν ἐφ' ἑαυτῇ μεγαλοφρονεῖν.
130 μηθὲν ὧν ἀφαιρήσεταί σε κακὸς ἀνὴρ τίμα.
131 μόνον ἀγαθὸν ἡγοῦ τὸ πρέπον θεῷ.
132 τὸ ἄξιον θεοῦ καὶ ἀνδρὸς ἀγαθοῦ.

113- Cf. Plato, *Rep.* 379B.
14
125 Om. Π.
127 Om. Π.
131 Cf. 197.

113   Consider God as the cause of whatever you do well.

114   God is not the cause of evil.

115   Do not acquire more than the body needs.

116   Gold does not rescue the soul from evil.

117   You were not born to luxuriate in what God provides.

118   Acquire those things which no one can take from you.

119   Bear with what must be as something that must be.

120   Practice magnanimity.

121a   Do not surround yourself with those things which, if
       you despised them, would rightfully bring you praise.

121b   Possess those things of which you are rightfully
       proud.

122   Pray to God for whatever is worthy of God.

123   Take your reason as a guide for your life.

124   Ask God for whatever you cannot get from man.

125   Ask as a reward for your hard effort those things
       which come only through hard effort.

126   The prayer of a lazy man is an empty word.

127   Despise whatever you will not need after your
       release from the body.

128   Do not request from God possessions you will not be
       able to keep.

129   Train your soul to value itself next to God.

130   Value nothing that an evil man can take from you.

131   Consider as good only what is suitable to God.

132   Whatever is worthy of God is also worthy of a good
       man.

32

133 ὃ οὐ συμβάλλεται πρὸς εὐδαιμονίαν θεῷ, οὐδὲ
ἀνθρώπῳ.

134 ταῦτα θέλε ἃ θέλοι ἂν καὶ ὁ θεός.

135 υἱὸς θεοῦ ὁ ταῦτα μόνα τιμῶν ἃ καὶ ὁ θεός.

136 ἐφ' ὅσον ποθεῖ τὸ σῶμα, ἡ ψυχὴ τὸν θεὸν ἀγνοεῖ.

137 ὄρεξις κτήσεως ἀρχὴ πλεονεξίας.

138 ἐκ φιλαυτίας ἀδικία φύεται.

139a ὀλίγα πέφυκεν τῇ ψυχῇ τὸ σῶμα ἐνοχλεῖν.

139b φιληδονία ποιεῖ σῶμα ἀφόρητον.

140 πᾶν τὸ πλέον ἀνθρώπῳ πολέμιον.

141 φιλῶν ἃ μὴ δεῖ οὐ φιλήσεις ἃ δεῖ.

142 σπουδάζοντά σε περὶ τὰ μὴ καλὰ λήσεται τὰ καλά.

143 σοφοῦ διάνοια ἀεὶ παρὰ θεῷ.

144 σοφοῦ διανοίᾳ θεὸς ἐνοικεῖ.

145 σοφὸς ὀλίγοις γινώσκεται.

146 ἀπλήρωτος ἐπιθυμία ἅπασα παντός, διὰ τοῦτο καὶ
ἄπορος.

147 τὸ σοφὸν ἀεὶ ἑαυτῷ ὅμοιον.

148 αὐτάρκες πρὸς εὐδαιμονίαν θεοῦ γνῶσις καὶ ὁμοίωμα.

149 κακοὶ κολακευόμενοι κακίους γίνονται.

150 ἀφόρητον γίνεται κακία ἐπαινουμένη.

151 ἡ γλῶσσά σου τῷ νοΐ σου ἐπέσθω.

---

133 οὐ] Y latt: om. Π / οὐδὲ] Y latt: καὶ Π.
138 ἐκ₂ . . . φύεται] latt Elt. Ch. (φιλαργυρίας
sy²--sic etiam Clitarchus 24): ἡ ἀδικία ἀδικία
γίνεται Y: ἐκ φιλαυτίας κακία φύεται Π.
145 Ante 143 pl. lat. Quoted without attribution in
the *Regula Magistri* 10 and the *Rule of St. Benedict*
7.
146 ἅπασα παντός] Π latt (om. παντός) Elt.: om. Y Ch.

133   Whatever does not contribute to God's happiness
      does not contribute to man's happiness.
134   Desire whatever God would also desire.
135   God's son is the one who values only what God also
      values.
136   As long as the body is filled with desire, the soul
      does not know God.
137   The beginning of avarice is a longing for possessions.
138   Injustice results from self-love.
139a The body by nature causes little disturbance for
      the soul.
139b Love of pleasure makes the body unbearable.
140   Every excess is an enemy of man.
141   If you love what you should not, you will not love
      what you should.
142   If you strive for what is base you will miss what
      is noble.
143   The sage's mind is always with God.
144   God dwells in the mind of a sage.
145   The sage is recognized by few.
146   Every kind of desire is insatiable and so remains
      unmanageable.
147   What is wise is always similar to itself.
148   Sufficient for happiness is the knowledge and
      imitation of God.
149   Flattery makes evil people even worse.
150   Approbation makes wickedness unbearable.
151   Let your tongue obey your mind.

152 αἱρετώτερον λίθον εἰκῇ βάλλειν ἢ λόγον.

153 σκέπτου πρὸ τοῦ λέγειν ἵνα μὴ λέγῃς ἃ μὴ δεῖ.

154 ῥήματα ἄνευ νοῦ ψόγος.

155 πολυλογία οὐκ ἐκφεύγει ἁμαρτίαν.

156 βραχυλογίᾳ σοφία παρακολουθεῖ.

157 μακρολογία σημεῖον ἀμαθίας.

158 τὸ ἀληθὲς ἀγάπα.

159 τῷ ψεύδει χρῶ ὡς φαρμάκῳ.

160 καιρὸς τῶν λόγων σου προηγείσθω.

161 λέγε ὅτε σιγᾶν οὐ καθήκει.

162a περὶ ὧν οὐκ οἶδας σιώπα.

162b περὶ ὧν οἶδας, ὅτε δεῖ λέγε.

163a λόγος παρὰ καιρὸν διανοίας ἔλεγχος κακῆς.

163b ὁπότε δεῖ πράττειν, λόγῳ μὴ χρῶ.

164a ἐν συλλόγῳ πρῶτος λέγειν μὴ ἐπιτήδευε.

164b ἡ αὐτὴ ἐπιστήμη ἐστὶ τοῦ λέγειν καὶ τοῦ σιωπᾶν.

165a ἄμεινον ἡττᾶσθαι τἀληθῆ λέγοντα τοῦ περιγενέσθαι
μετὰ ἀπάτης.

165b ὁ νικῶν τῷ ἀπατᾶν νικᾶται ἐν ἤθει.

165c μάρτυρες κακῶν γίνονται λόγοι ψευδεῖς.

165d μεγάλη περίστασις ᾗ πρέπει ψεῦδος.

165e ὁπότε ἁμαρτάνων εἶ τἀληθῆ λέγων, ἀναγκαίως
τότε ψευδῆ λέγων οὐχ ἁμαρτήσεις.

165f μηδένα ἀπάτα, μάλιστα τον συμβουλίας δεόμενον.

165g μετὰ πλειόνων λέγων μᾶλλον ὄψει τὰ συμφέροντα.

---

152 Attributed to Origen in *Regula Magistri* 11.
154 ψόγος] Π latt: φόβος Υ: ψόφοι coni. Elt.
(secundum Clitarchus 30): ψόφος coni. Ch.
155 ἐκφεύγει] Π syy: ἐκφεύξῃ Υ latt. Cf. Prov. 10.19:
ἐκ πολυλογίας οὐκ ἐκφεύξῃ ἁμαρτίαν.
157 Om. Υ. Incipit copt.
159 Coniungitur 159 cum 158 (ⲁⲅⲱ) copt. Φάρμακον can
mean "poison" (so copt, latt, sy²) but also
"medicinal remedy" (so sy¹).
162a Om. copt (haplography).
162b ὧν] Π Υ: ὧν δὲ copt latt (sy²?).
163b Om. Π latt.
164b ἡ . . . σιωπᾶν] copt sy² (Gk. coni. Elt. secundum
Clitarchus 38): om. Π Υ latt.
165b Om. Π latt / ἤθει] Υ (sy¹?): ἀληθείᾳ copt sy².
165c-g Om. Π latt.

152 It is better to toss a stone without purpose
     than a word.
153 Think carefully before speaking lest you say things
     that you should not.
154 Words without thought deserve reproach.
155 Excessive talking cannot avoid sin.
156 Wisdom accompanies brevity of speech.
157 Speaking at length is a sign of ignorance.
158 Love the truth.
159 Treat a lie like poison.
160 Let the opportune moment guide your words.
161 Speak when it is not right to keep silent.
162a Be silent about what you do not know.
162b Speak when you should about what you do know.
163a An untimely word is proof of an evil mind.
163b Do not talk when action is required.
164a In an assembly do not strive to speak first.
164b Speaking and being silent require the same level
     of understanding.
165a It is better to speak the truth and lose than to win
     with deception.
165b Whoever wins with deception loses his integrity.
165c False words are attestations of evil.
165d It is a drastic situation in which a lie is
     appropriate.
165e When you would sin by speaking the truth, then you
     would surely not sin by speaking untruthfully.
165f Deceive no one, least of all one who seeks advice.
165g By consulting many people you will better recognize
     what is beneficial.

36

166 πιστὸς ἁπασῶν καλῶν πράξεων ἡγεμών ἐστιν.
167 σοφία ψυχὴν ὁδηγεῖ πρὸς θεόν.
168 οὐδὲν οἰκειότερον σοφίᾳ ἀληθείας.
169 οὐ δυνατὸν τὴν αὐτὴν φύσιν πιστήν τε εἶναι καὶ
     φιλοψευδῆ.
170 δειλῇ καὶ ἀνελευθέρῳ φύσει πίστις οὐκ ἂν μετείη.
171a τὸ λέγειν ἃ δεῖ τοῦ ἀκούειν πιστὸς ὢν μὴ προτίμα.
171b ἐν πιστοῖς ὧν μᾶλλον ἄκουε ἤπερ λέγε.
172 φιλήδονος ἀνὴρ ἄχρηστος ἐν παντί.
173 ἀνεύθυνος ὢν λόγοις χρῶ περὶ θεοῦ.
174 τὰ τῶν ἀγνοούντων ἁμαρτήματα τῶν διδαξάντων αὐτοὺς
     ὀνείδη.
175 νεκροὶ παρὰ θεῷ δι᾽ οὓς τὸ ὄνομα τοῦ θεοῦ λοιδορεῖται.
176 σοφὸς ἀνὴρ εὐεργέτης μετὰ θεόν.
177 τοὺς λόγους σου ὁ βίος βεβαιούτω παρὰ τοῖς ἀκούουσιν.
178 ὃ μὴ δεῖ ποιεῖν, μηδ᾽ ὑπονοοῦ ποιεῖν.
179 ἃ μὴ θέλεις παθεῖν, μηδὲ ποίει.
180 ἃ ποιεῖν αἰσχρόν, καὶ προστάττειν ἑτέρῳ αἰσχρόν.
181 μέχρι καὶ τοῦ νοῦ καθάρευε τῶν ἁμαρτημάτων.
182 ἄρχων ἀνθρώπων μέμνησο ἄρχεσθαι παρὰ θεοῦ.
183 ὁ κρίνων ἄνθρωπον κρίνεται ὑπὸ τοῦ θεοῦ.

---

166 πιστὸς] Π Υ: πίστις latt sy² Elt.Ch./ καλῶν] Υ
     copt sy²: τῶν Π latt.
172 φιλήδονος] Π copt latt syy: ἄπιστος Υ.
173 λόγοις χρῶ] Υ latt sy²: λόγοις μὴ χρῶ Π Elt. Ch.
175 Cf. Rom 2.24.
178 ὑπονοοῦ] Υ latt: ὑπονόει copt sy²: ὑποπτεύου
     ποιεῖν μήτε ὑπονόει₂Π sy¹.
180 ἑτέρῳ αἰσχρόν] Υ sy²: ἄλλῳ αἰσχρότερόν ἐστιν Π
     (latt?). Hic desinit copt.
183 Om. Υ. Cf. Mt. 7.1 / Lk 6.37.

166 The faithful person is a guide for every good deed.

167 Wisdom leads a soul to God.

168 Nothing is closer to wisdom than truth.

169 One and the same nature cannot be both faithful and fond of deceit.

170 Faith could not have anything in common with a cowardly and servile nature.

171a Since you are faithful, do not prefer speaking things which you should be hearing.

171b When among believers listen rather than speak.

172 A man fond of pleasure is useless in every respect.

173 Speak about God only if you are blameless.

174 The sins of the ignorant are a reproach to their teachers.

175 Dead in God's sight are those who cause God's name to be reviled.

176 The wise man is a benefactor second only to God.

177 Let your way of life confirm your words among those who hear you.

178 Do not even think about doing what should not be done.

179 What you do not want to experience, do not do.

180 What is shameful to do is also shameful to require of someone else.

181 Even in your thoughts, purify yourself of sins.

182 In governing human beings remember that you are governed by God.

183 Whoever judges a human being is himself judged by God.

38

184 μείζων ὁ κίνδυνος δικαζομένου δικαστῇ.
185 ἅπασι μᾶλλον ἢ λόγῳ βλάπτε ἄνθρωπον.
186 δυνατὸν ἀπατῆσαι λόγῳ ἄνθρωπον, θεὸν μέντοι
ἀδύνατον.
187 οὐ χαλεπὸν ἐπίστασθαι καὶ ἐν λόγῳ νενικῆσθαι.
188 κακοδοξίας αἰτιώτατον ἡ ἐν πίστει φιλοδοξία.
189 τίμα τὸ πιστὸς εἶναι διὰ τοῦ εἶναι.
190 σέβου σοφὸν ἄνδρα ὡς εἰκόνα θεοῦ ζῶσαν.
191 σοφὸς ἀνὴρ καὶ γυμνὸς ὢν δοκείτω σοι σοφὸς εἶναι.
192 διὰ τὸ πολλὰ ἔχειν χρήματα ⟨μὴ⟩ τιμήσῃς μηδένα.
193 χαλεπόν ἐστιν πλουτοῦντα σωθῆναι.
194 ψέγειν ἄνδρα σοφὸν καὶ θεὸν ἴσον ἁμάρτημα.

195 λόγον χειρίζων περὶ θεοῦ παραθήκην σοι δεδόσθαι
νόμιζε τὰς ψυχὰς τῶν ἀκουόντων.
196 οὐκ ἔστιν βιῶναι καλῶς μὴ πεπιστευκότα γνησίως.
197 μόνον τὸ καλὸν ἀγαθὸν ἡγοῦ καὶ καλὸν μόνον τὸ
πρέπον θεῷ.
198 ποίει μεγάλα μὴ μεγάλα ὑπισχνούμενος.
199 οὐ γενήσῃ σοφὸς οἰόμενος εἶναι πρὸ τοῦ εἶναι.

200 μεγάλη περίστασις πιστὸν ἄνδρα δείκνυσι.
201 τέλος ἡγοῦ βίου τὸ ζῆν κατὰ θεόν.
202 μηδὲν ἡγοῦ κακόν, ὃ μή ἐστιν αἰσχρόν.

203 κακοῦ πέρας ὕβρις, ὕβρεως δὲ ὄλεθρος.

204 οὐκ ἀναβήσεται πάθος ἐπὶ καρδίαν πιστοῦ.
205 πᾶν πάθος ψυχῆς λόγῳ πολέμιον.
206 ὃ ἂν πράξῃς ἐν πάθει ὤν, μετανοήσεις.

---

192 ⟨μὴ⟩] coni. Lloyd-Jones.
193 Cf. Mt. 19.23 / Mk. 10.23 / Lk. 18.24.
197 Cf. 131.
201 Cf. I Pet. 4.6.
202 Coniungitur cum 203 Π lat[WT].
203 κακοῦ] Π Y latt Elt.: κόρου sy[2] Ch.

184 There is greater danger in judging than in being
    judged.

185 Hurt a person with anything but words.

186 If you can deceive a person with words, you cannot
    so deceive God.

187 It is no misfortune to have knowledge and yet to
    lose an argument.

188 In matters of faith, the love of renown usually
    causes the loss of renown.

189 Honor faithfulness by being faithful.

190 Respect the wise man as a living image of God.

191 You should consider the wise man to be wise even
    when he is naked.

192 Do not honor anyone on the basis of his many
    possessions.

193 It is difficult for the rich man to be saved.

194 It is as sinful to find fault with a wise man as to
    find fault with God.

195 When you attempt to speak about God, consider that
    the souls of your listeners have been entrusted
    to you.

196 It is not possible to live well if you do not truly
    have faith.

197 Consider only what is noble to be good and only what
    befits God to be noble.

198 Do great things rather than promise them.

199 You will never become wise if you think you are wise
    before you really are.

200 A drastic situation reveals the man of faith.

201 Consider the purpose of life to live according to God.

202 Whatever is not shameful, do not consider evil.

203 The result of evil is insolence, and the result of
    insolence is destruction.

204 Passion will not arise in the heart of a faithful
    person.

205 Every passion of the soul is an enemy of reason.

206 Whatever you do out of passion you will regret.

40

207	πάθη νοσημάτων ἀρχαί.
208a	κακία νόσος ψυχῆς.
208b	ἀδικία ψυχῆς θάνατος.
209	τότε δόκει πιστὸς εἶναι, ὅταν τῶν τῆς ψυχῆς παθῶν ἀπαλλαγῆς.
210a	ἀνθρώποις χρῶ τοῖς ἅπασιν ὡς κοινὸς ἀνθρώπων εὐεργέτης.
210b	ὡς θέλεις χρήσασθαί σοι τοὺς πέλας, καὶ σὺ χρῶ αὐτοῖς.
211	ἀνθρώποις κακῶς χρώμενος σεαυτῷ κακῶς χρήσῃ.
212	οὐδένα κακῶς ποιήσει ὁ πιστός.
213	εὔχου τοὺς ἐχθροὺς δύνασθαι εὐεργετεῖν.
214	φαύλοις φαίνεται ἄχρηστος σοφὸς ἀνήρ.
215	οὐκ ἄνευ θεοῦ καλῶς ζήσεις.
216	ὑπὲρ τοῦ κατὰ θεὸν ζῆν πάντα ὑπόμενε.
217	εὐχῆς οὐκ ἀκούει θεὸς τοῦ ἀνθρώπων δεομένων οὐκ ἀκούοντος.
218	φιλόσοφος φιλοσόφῳ δῶρον παρὰ θεοῦ.
219	τιμῶν φιλόσοφον τιμήσεις σεαυτόν.
220	πιστὸς ὢν ἴσθι.
221	ὅταν υἱόν σε λέγῃ τις, μέμνησο τίνος σε λέγει υἱόν.
222	θεὸν πατέρα καλῶν ἐν οἷς πράττεις τούτου μέμνησο.
223	τὰ ῥήματα σου τὰ πιστὰ πολλῆς εὐσεβείας μεστὰ ἔστω.
224	ἐν οἷς πράττεις πρὸ ὀφθαλμῶν ἔχε τὸν θεόν.
225	δεινόν ἐστιν θεὸν πατέρα ὁμολογοῦντα πρᾶξαί τι ἄσχημον.

208a Om. Y.
210b = 89. Post 212 Y: om. latt. Cf. Mt. 7.12 / Lk. 6.31.
211   Om. Y (sy²: invenitur apud 219?).
213   Cf. Mt. 5.44 / Lk. 6.27-28.
222   = 59.
223   τὰ πιστά] Π Y Elt.: om. latt sy² (bracketed by
      Ch.) / εὐσεβείας] Π latt (sy²?): εὐλαβείας Y.

207 Chief among illnesses are passions.

208a Wickedness is a disease of the soul.

208b Injustice is the death of the soul.

209 Consider yourself to be faithful only when you put aside the passions of the soul.

210a Treat all human beings as though you were a public benefactor of humanity.

210b As you want your neighbors to treat you, so treat them.

211 In mistreating human beings, you mistreat yourself.

212 The faithful person will not act badly toward anyone.

213 Pray that you may be able to do good to your enemies.

214 A wise man appears useless to the masses.

215 You will not live well without God.

216 Endure everything in order to live according to God.

217 God does not heed the prayer of a man who does not listen to the needy.

218 To a philosopher a philosopher is a gift from God.

219 If you honor a philosopher, you will honor yourself.

220 Live as a believer.

221 When someone calls you "son," remember Whose son he calls you.

222 You call God "Father": remember this in your actions.

223 Let your words of faith be full of great piety.

224 In whatever you do, keep God before your eyes.

225 It is dreadful while confessing God as Father to do something shameful.

42

226 σοφὸν ὁ μὴ φιλῶν, οὐδὲ ἑαυτόν.

227 μηθὲν ἴδιον κτῆμα νομιζέσθω φιλοσόφῳ.

228 ὧν κοινὸς ὁ θεὸς καὶ ταῦτα ὡς πατήρ, τούτων μὴ
      κοινὰ εἶναι τὰ κτήματα οὐκ εὐσεβές.

229 ἀχαριστεῖ θεῷ ὁ μὴ περὶ πολλοῦ ποιούμενος φιλόσοφον.

230a γάμον δίδωσίν σοι παραιτεῖσθαι ἵνα ζήσῃς ὡς πάρεδρος
      θεῷ.

230b γάμει καὶ παιδοποιοῦ χαλεπὸν εἰδὼς ἑκάτερον· εἰ
      δὲ καθάπερ εἰδὼς πόλεμον ὅτι χαλεπὸν ἀνδρίζοιο,
      καὶ γάμει καὶ παιδοποιοῦ.

231 μοιχὸς τῆς ἑαυτοῦ γυναικὸς πᾶς ὁ ἀκόλαστος.

232 μηδὲν ἕνεκα ψιλῆς ἡδονῆς ποίει.

233 ἴσθι μοιχὸς εἶναι κἂν νοήσῃς μοιχεῦσαι· καὶ περὶ
      παντὸς ἁμαρτήματος ὁ αὐτὸς ἔστω σοι λόγος.

234 πιστὸν εἰπὼν σεαυτὸν ὡμολόγησας μηδὲ ἁμαρτεῖν
      θεῷ.

235 πιστῇ γυναικὶ κόσμος σωφροσύνη νομιζέσθω.

236 ἀνὴρ γυναῖκα ἀποπέμπων ὁμολογεῖ μηδὲ γυναικὸς
      ἄρχειν δύνασθαι.

237 γυνὴ σώφρων ἀνδρὸς εὔκλεια.

238 αἰδούμενος γαμετὴν αἰδουμένην ἕξεις.

239 ὁ τῶν πιστῶν γάμος ἀγὼν ἔστω περὶ ἐγκρατείας.

240 ὡς ἂν γαστρὸς ἄρξῃς, καὶ ἀφροδισίων ἄρξεις.

---

228 Om. Y sy^2.
230a γάμον] Π latt sy^2: γάμον γὰρ Y Elt. Ch. (The γὰρ
      is probably secondary, a redactional joining of
      230a with 229.)
230b γάμει . . . ἑκάτερον] Π latt: om. Y sy^2.
231 Cited by Jerome (*Adv. Iovin.* 1.49 and *In Ezech.* 6.18).
232 μηδὲν] Y latt: μηδὲ Π.
233 ἴσθι . . . μοιχεῦσαι] Y latt sy^1: μοιχὸς ὢν ἴσθι
      εἶναι κἂν νοσεῖς τὸ μοιχεύειν Π. Cf. Mt. 5.28.
235 Post 235 sequuntur 262, 379-405, dein 236-61 Π.

226   Whoever does not love a sage does not love
even himself.

227   Let the philosopher not think of anything as his
own property.

228   It is impious for those who share God in common, and
indeed as Father, not to share possessions in common.

229   Whoever does not esteem the philosopher is ungrateful to God.

230a   It is allowed to you to renounce marriage so that
you might live as a companion of God.

230b   Marry and beget children knowing that both are
difficult; if you know this, as you know that a
battle could be hard and that you would be brave,
then marry and have children.

231   Every unrestrained husband commits adultery with
his wife.

232   Do nothing for the sake of mere sensual pleasure.

233   Know that you are an adulterer even if you merely
think of committing adultery. And let your
attitude about every sin be the same.

234   In calling yourself a believer, you have pledged that
you will not sin against God.

235   Let moderation be the normal attire of a believing
wife.

236   A man who divorces his wife admits that he is not
even able to govern a woman.

237   A modest wife is her husband's glory.

238   If you respect your wife, you will keep her
respect.

239   Let the marriage of believers be a struggle for
self-control.

240   As you control your stomach, so you will control
your sexual desires.

44

241 φυλάττου τὸν παρὰ τῶν ἀπίστων ἔπαινον.
242 ἃ προῖκα λαμβάνεις παρὰ θεοῦ, καὶ δίδου προῖκα.
243 πλῆθος πιστῶν οὐκ ἂν ἐξεύροις· σπάνιον γὰρ τὸ ἀγαθόν.
244 σοφὸν τίμα μετὰ θεόν.
245 ἐλεγχόμενος ἵνα γένῃ σοφὸς χάριν ἴσθι τοῖς
    ἐλέγχουσιν.
246 ὁ τὸν σοφὸν οὐ δυνάμενος φέρειν τὸ ἀγαθὸν οὐ δύναται
    φέρειν.
247 πιστὸς εἶναι θέλων μάλιστα μὲν μὴ ἁμάρτῃς, εἰ δέ
    τι, μὴ δισσῶς τὸ αὐτό.
248 ὃ μή ἐστι μάθημα θεοῦ ἄξιον, μὴ μάθῃς.
249 πολυμαθία περιεργία ψυχῆς νομιζέσθω.
250 ὁ τὰ τοῦ θεοῦ ἀξίως εἰδὼς σοφὸς ἀνήρ.
251 χωρὶς μαθήματος οὐκ ἔσῃ θεοφιλής· ἐκείνου περιέχου
    ὡς ἀναγκαίου.
252 φείδεται χρόνου σοφὸς ἀνήρ.
253a παρρησίαν ἄγε μετὰ αἰδοῦς.
253b ἔστιν σοφοῦ καὶ ὕπνος ἐγκράτεια.
254 ἀνιάτω σε μᾶλλον τέκνα κακῶς ζῶντα τοῦ μὴ ζῆν.
255 τὸ γὰρ ζῆν μὲν οὐκ ἐφ᾽ ἡμῖν, καλῶς δὲ ζῆν καὶ ἐφ᾽ ἡμῖν.

256 τέκνα μὴ πιστὰ οὐ τέκνα.
257 πιστὸς ἀνὴρ εὐχαρίστως φέρει τέκνων ἀποβολήν.
258 μὴ κρίνῃς φιλόσοφον ᾧ μὴ πάντα πιστεύεις.
259 διαβολὰς κατὰ φιλοσόφου μὴ παραδέχου.

---

242   Cf. Mt. 10.8.
247   Om. Π. Cf. Sir. 7.8.
253a ἄγε] Π latt: ἄγει Υ sy².

241   Be wary of the approval of non-believers.
242   What you freely receive from God, freely give.
243   You will not find a multitude of belicvers, for
      goodness is rare.
244   After God, honor the sage.
245   When people rebuke you to make you wise, be
      grateful to them.
246   Whoever is unable to endure a sage is unable to
      endure goodness.
247   If you wish to be faithful, above all do not sin.
      However, if you do sin, do not commit the same sin
      twice.
248   Do not study a teaching which is unworthy of God.
249   Recognize that too much learning is superfluous
      for the soul.
250   He who knows in a worthy manner the things of God
      is a wise man.
251   Without learning you cannot be a person who loves
      God; accept learning as necessary.
252   A wise man is thrifty with his time.
253a Use freedom of speech with reserve.
253b For the sage even sleep is a matter for self-control.
254   You should be more distressed about children who
      live wickedly than about children who are no longer
      living.
255   For we cannot control the length of life, but we
      can control whether we live properly.
256   If children do not believe, they are not children.
257   The man of faith bears the loss of his children
      thankfully.
258   Do not accept someone as a philosopher unless you
      trust him completely.
259   Do not allow a philosopher to be slandered.

46

260 ἐπιτήδευε κοινὸς ἀνθρώποις εὐεργέτης εἶναι.
261 ἀπευκτὸν ἡγοῦ καὶ τὸ δικαίως τινὰ κολάζειν.
262 μετ᾽ εὐθυμίας εἰ θέλεις ζῆν, μὴ πολλὰ πρᾶττε·
πολυπραγμονῶν γὰρ κακοπραγμονῶν ἔσῃ.
263 ὃ μὴ κατέθου, μηδ᾽ ἀνέλῃς, οὐ γὰρ κατὰ τὸν αὐτάρκη
πολιτεύῃ.
264a ἀφεὶς ἃ κέκτησαι ἀκολούθει τῷ ὀρθῷ λόγῳ.
264b ἐλεύθερος ἔσῃ ἀπὸ πάντων δουλεύων θεῷ.
265 ἀπαλλάττου τροφῆς ἔτι θέλων.
266 τροφῆς παντὶ κοινώνει.
267 ὑπὲρ τοῦ πτωχὸν τραφῆναι καὶ νηστεῦσαι καλόν.
268 ποτόν σοι πᾶν ἡδὺ ἔστω.
269 μέθην δὲ ὁμοίως μανίᾳ φυλάττου.
270 ἄνθρωπος γαστρὸς ἡττώμενος ὅμοιος θηρίῳ.
271 οὐδὲν φύεται ἐκ σαρκὸς ἀγαθόν.
272 αἰσχρᾶς ἡδονῆς τὸ μὲν ἡδὺ ταχέως ἄπεισιν, τὸ δὲ
ὄνειδος παραμένει.
273 ἀνθρώπους ἴδοις ἂν ὑπὲρ τοῦ τὸ λοιπὸν τοῦ σώματος
ἔχειν ἐρρωμένον ἀποκόπτοντας ἑαυτῶν καὶ ῥίπτοντας
μέλη· πόσῳ βέλτιον ὑπὲρ τοῦ σωφρονεῖν;
274a μεγάλην νόμιζε παιδείαν τὸ ἄρχειν σώματος·
274b οὐ γὰρ παύσει ἐπιθυμίαν κτημάτων ἢ χρημάτων κτῆσις.
275 φιλόσοφον οὐδέν ἐστιν ὃ τῆς ἐλευθερίας ἀφαιρεῖται.

---

261 Post 261 sequuntur 428-30 Π.
263 The first part is attributed to Solon (Diogenes
Laertius 1.57) and also appears in Plato (*Laws* 913C).
264 Cf. Mt. 19.21 / Mk. 10.21 / Lk. 18.22.
268 Attributed to Socrates (Xenophon, *Mem.* 1.3.5).
271 σαρκὸς] Υ latt: γαστρὸς Π sy². Cf. Rom. 7.18,
Gal. 6.8.
273 καὶ ῥίπτοντας] Π sy¹ Orig. (*Comm. in Matt.* 15:3):
om. Υ latt / μέλη] Υ: τὰ μέλη Π: μέρη Orig.
[The probable biblical influence on the mss. tradition
of Sextus 13 is less likely here.]
274b γὰρ] Π pm. lat sy²: om. Υ lat^GU.

260 Strive to be a public benefactor to humanity.

261 Consider even the just punishment of someone to be abominable.

262 If you want to live happily, do not do too many things; for if you do more than you should, you will do it poorly.

263 Do not collect more than you have deposited, for in so doing you do not live in accord with self-sufficiency.

264a Let go of your possessions and follow the right teaching.

264b You will be free from all things if you serve God.

265 Stop eating while you still desire more food.

266 Share your food with everyone.

267 In order to provide food for the poor it is good even to fast.

268 Let every drink be pleasing to you.

269 However, ward off drunkenness as you would madness.

270 A man ruled by his stomach is like an animal.

271 Nothing good derives from the flesh.

272 The sweetness of disgraceful pleasure swiftly departs but the reproach remains.

273 You may see men who, in order to keep the rest of their bodies healthy, cut off their own limbs and throw them away. Is it not much better to do that for the sake of self-control?

274a Consider the control of the body to be an important accomplishment.

274b For the possession of goods will not stop a longing for possessions.

275 Nothing exists which deprives a philosopher of his freedom.

48

276 ἡδονὰς ἡγοῦ τὰς ἀναγκαίας ὡς ἀναγκαίας.
277 τὰ ἀγαθὰ μὲν ἔχειν πάντες εὔχονται, κτῶνται δὲ οἱ
γνησίως τοῦ θείου λόγου μετέχοντες.
278 φιλόσοφος ὢν σεμνὸς ἔσο μᾶλλον ἢ φιλοσκώπτης.
279 σπάνιόν σου ἔστω σκῶμμα καὶ τὸ εὔκαιρον.
280a ἄμετρος γέλως σημεῖον ἀπροσεξίας.
280b σεαυτῷ διαχεῖσθαι πέρα τοῦ μειδιᾶν μὴ ἐπιτρέψῃς.
281 σπουδῇ πλείονι ἢ διαχύσει χρῶ.
282 ἀγὼν ὁ βίος ἔστω σοι περὶ τοῦ σεμνοῦ.
283 ἄριστον μὲν τὸ μὴ ἁμαρτεῖν, ἁμαρτάνοντα δὲ γινώσκειν
ἄμεινον ἢ ἀγνοεῖν.
284 ἀλαζὼν φιλόσοφος οὐκ ἔστιν.
285 μεγάλην σοφίαν νόμιζε δι' ἧς δυνήσῃ φέρειν ἀγνοούντων
ἀπαιδευσίαν.
286 αἰσχρὸν ἡγοῦ λόγον ἔχων διὰ στόμα ἐπαινεῖσθαι.
287 σοφῶν ψυχαὶ ἀκόρεστοι θεοσεβείας.
288 ἀρχόμενος ἀπὸ θεοῦ πρᾶττε ὃ ἂν πράττῃς.
289 συνεχέστερον νόει τὸν θεὸν ἢ ἀνάπνει.
290 ἃ μαθόντα δεῖ ποιεῖν, ἄνευ τοῦ μαθεῖν μὴ ἐπιχείρει.
291 σαρκὸς μὴ ἔρα.
292 ψυχῆς ἀγαθῆς ἔρα μετὰ θεόν.
293 οἰκείων ὀργὰς δύνασθαι φέρειν κατὰ φιλόσοφον.
294 φιλοσόφου πλοῦτος ἐγκράτεια.

276 Ante 274 Y.
279 Om. Π.
280b Cf. Sir. 21.20.
282 = 573. τοῦ σεμνοῦ] Y (573) sy¹ (latt?) Ch.:
βίου σεμνοῦ Π Y Elt. (sed vide notam eius).
286 στόμα] Π latt Ch.: σῶμα Y sy² Elt.
289 Cited by Gregory Nazianzen (Orat. Theol. 1[27]. 4).
294 φιλοσόφου] syy Elt.: φιλοσόφω Π: φιλοσόφων
pl. lat: πιστοῦ Y (cf. 319) Ch.

276 Consider unavoidable pleasures to be necessary.

277 All people pray to have good things, but those who truly have a share in divine reason acquire them.

278 If you are a philosopher, be a serious rather than a frivolous person.

279 Let your light-heartedness be both rare and timely.

280a Immoderate laughter is a sign of inattentiveness.

280b Do not allow yourself more levity than a smile.

281 Display seriousness more often than levity.

282 Let your life be a struggle for seriousness.

283 It is best not to sin, but if you do sin, it is better to acknowledge it than to ignore it.

284 A philosopher is not a braggart.

285 Consider that wisdom to be great by which you are able to bear the lack of learning of the ignorant.

286 As a reasonable person, consider it shameful to be praised in public.

287 The souls of the sages have an insatiable desire to serve God.

288 Do whatever you do under God's control.

289 Think about God more often than you breathe.

290 Whatever should be done only with instruction, do not attempt without instruction.

291 Do not love the flesh.

292 After God, love a noble soul.

293 The ability to endure the anger of friends is in accord with philosophy.

294 Self-control is the wealth of a philosopher.

50

295 ὅπερ μεταδιδοὺς ἄλλοις αὐτὸς οὐχ ἕξεις, μὴ κρίνῃς
     ἀγαθὸν εἶναι.
296 οὐδὲν ἀκοινώνητον ἀγαθόν.
297a μὴ νόμιζε μικρότερον ἁμάρτημα ἄλλο ἄλλου.
[297b πᾶν ἁμάρτημα ἀσέβημα ἡγοῦ.]
298 ὡς ἐπὶ τοῖς κατορθώμασιν ἐπαινεῖσθαι θέλεις, καὶ
     ἐπὶ τοῖς ἁμαρτήμασιν ψεγόμενος ἀνέχου.
299 ὧν τῶν ἐπαίνων καταφρονεῖς, καὶ τῶν ψόγων ὑπερόρα.
300 θησαυρὸν κατατίθεσθαι μὲν οὐ φιλάνθρωπον, ἀναιρεῖσθαι
     δὲ οὐ κατὰ φιλόσοφον.
301 ὅσα πονεῖς διὰ τὸ σῶμα, καὶ διὰ τὴν ψυχὴν πονέσας
     σοφὸς ἂν εἴης.
302 σοφὸν οὐδέν ἐστιν ὃ βλάπτει.
303 ὧν ἂν πράττῃς θεὸν ἐπικαλοῦ μάρτυρα.
304 ὁ θεὸς ἀνθρώπων βεβαιοῖ καλὰς πράξεις.
305 κακῶν πράξεων κακὸς δαίμων ἡγεμών ἐστιν.
306 οὐκ ἀναγκάσεις σοφὸν πρᾶξαι ὃ μὴ βούλεται μᾶλλον
     ἤπερ θεόν.
307 σοφὸς ἀνὴρ θεὸν ἀνθρώποις συνιστᾷ.
308 ὁ θεὸς τῶν ἰδίων ἔργων μέγιστον φρονεῖ ἐπὶ σοφῷ.
309 οὐδὲν οὕτως ἐλεύθερον μετὰ θεὸν ὡς σοφὸς ἀνήρ.
310 ὅσα θεοῦ κτήματα, καὶ σοφοῦ.
311 κοινωνεῖ βασιλείας θεοῦ σοφὸς ἀνήρ.

297b = 11. Om. Π latt syy.
298   ἐπαινεῖσθαι] latt sy²: ἐπαινεῖσθαι καὶ τιμᾶσθαι
      Υ Elt.: τιμᾶσθαι Π Ch.
301   πονεῖς] coni. Elt. (cf. latt sy²): πονέσας Π Υ.
304   ἀνθρώπων] Π latt: ἀνθρώποις Υ sy².
307   Hic iterum incipit copt.
308   Wisse (NHL, p. 455) legit ⲁⲅⲱ ⲡⲛⲟⲩⲧ]ⲉ apud initium
      et sic coniungit 308 cum 307. Sed linea ms. hoc in
      loco solum 5-6 litteris caret.
309   οὐδὲν οὕτως ἐλεύθερον] Π Υ (sy²?): nihil tale verum
      latt (nihil tam liberum coni. Elt.): οὐδεὶς οὕτως
      ἐλεύθερος copt.
310   Om. Υ.
311   Om. Υ latᴳᵁ. Post 310 Π copt latᵂᵀ sy²: ante 310
      pm. lat / κοινωνεῖ βασιλείας] coni. Elt.: κοινωνοῖ
      βασιλεία Π.

295 Do not consider anything good which you cannot
    share with others and still have yourself.
296 Nothing is good which is not shared.
297a Do not consider one sin smaller than another.
297b Consider every sin a sacrilege.
298 As you desire to be commended for your upright
    deeds, so expect to be blamed for your sins.
299 Disregard the censures of those whose praises you
    despise.
300 To hoard riches is inhumane, but even to accept
    riches is contrary to philosophy.
301 If you endure as much for the soul as you endure
    for the body, you will be wise.
302 Nothing exists which is harmful to a sage.
303 In whatever you do, call upon God as witness.
304 God confirms the good deeds of human beings.
305 An evil demon guides evil deeds.
306 No more than you can compel God can you compel a
    sage to do what he does not wish.
307 A wise man presents God to humanity.
308 Of all his works God is most proud of a sage.
309 Next to God, nothing is as free as a wise man.
310 Whatever God possesses belongs also to the sage.
311 A wise man shares in the kingdom of God.

312 κακὸς ἀνὴρ πρόνοιαν θεοῦ εἶναι οὐ θέλει.

313 ψυχὴ κακὴ θεὸν φεύγει.

314 πᾶν τὸ φαῦλον θεῷ πολέμιον.

315 τὸ ἐν σοὶ φρονοῦν τοῦτο νόμιζε εἶναι ἄνθρωπον.

316 ὅπου σου τὸ φρονοῦν, ἐκεῖ σου τὸ ἀγαθόν.

317 ἀγαθὸν ἐν σαρκὶ μὴ ἐπιζήτει.

318 ὃ μὴ βλάπτει ψυχήν, οὐδὲ ἄνθρωπον.

319 φιλόσοφον ἄνθρωπον ὡς ὑπηρέτην θεοῦ τίμα μετὰ θεόν.

320 τὸ σκήνωμα τῆς ψυχῆς σου βαρύνεσθαι μὲν ὑπερήφανον,
     ἀποθέσθαι δὲ πραέως ὁπότε χρὴ δύνασθαι μακάριον.

321 θανάτου μὲν σαυτῷ παραίτιος μὴ γένῃ, τῷ δὲ ἀφαιρουμένῳ
     σε τοῦ σώματος μὴ ἀγανάκτει.

322 σοφὸν ὁ τοῦ σώματος ἀφαιρούμενος βίᾳ τῇ ἑαυτοῦ κακίᾳ
     εὐεργετεῖ, λύεται γὰρ ὡς ἐκ δεσμῶν.

---

313 Om. Y.
316 ἐκεῖ] Π Y copt: ἐκεῖ καὶ latt sy².
318 οὐδὲ] Y copt: οὔτε Π.
319 φιλόσοφον] Π latt: πιστὸν Y (cf. 294) [Deficit copt.]
320 τὸ . . . σου] Π (om. σου) Y: τὸ σκήνωμα τοῦ σώματος
     latt: τὰ κενώματα (?) τοῦ σώματος σου sy²: τὸ
     σῶμα τῆς [ψυχῆς] σου copt.
321 τῷ . . . σώματος] add. copt "and kills you"
     (ⲛ̄ϥⲙⲟⲟⲩⲧⲕ̄).
322 βίᾳ] copt latt (vi latS: iniuste rell.) sy² (sy¹?):
     om. Π Y Elt. Ch.

312 An evil man would deny God's providence.

313 An evil soul flees from God.

314 Everything base is inimical to God.

315 Consider your reason to be the essence of humanity.

316 Where your reason is, there is your good.

317 Do not seek goodness in flesh.

318 Whatever does not harm a soul, does not harm a man.

319 After God, honor the philosopher as a servant of God.

320 It is arrogant to be vexed by the tent of your soul, but it is blessed to be able to put it aside gently when you must.

321 Do not cause your own death, but do not be angry with the person who would deprive you of your body.

322 Whoever by his own wickedness forcibly deprives a sage of his body benefits him, for he releases him as though from chains.

323 ἄνθρωπον θανάτου φόβος λυπεῖ ἀπειρίᾳ ψυχῆς.

324 σίδηρον ἀνδροφόνον ἄριστον μὲν ἦν μὴ γενέσθαι,
γενόμενον δὲ σοὶ μὴ νόμιζε εἶναι.

325 οὐδεμία προσποίησις ἐπὶ πολὺν χρόνον λανθάνει,
μάλιστα δὲ ἐν πίστει.

326a οἷον ἐὰν ᾖ σου τὸ ἦθος, τοιοῦτος ἔσται σου καὶ ὁ
βίος.

326b ἦθος θεοσεβὲς ποιεῖ βίον μακάριον.

327 ὁ βουλευόμενος κατ᾽ ἄλλου κακῶς, φθάνει κακῶς πάσχων.

328 μή σε παύσῃ τοῦ εὐεργετεῖν ἀχάριστος ἄνθρωπος.

329 μηθὲν ὧν παραχρῆμα αἰτούμενος δῷς, πλείονος ἄξιον
κρίνῃς τοῦ λαμβάνοντος.

330 κάλλιστα οὐσίᾳ χρήσῃ τοῖς δεομένοις προθύμως μεταδι-
δούς.

331 ἀδελφὸν ἀγνωμονοῦντα πεῖθε μὴ ἀγνωμονεῖν καὶ ἀνιάτως
ἔχοντα συντήρει.

---

325 ἐπὶ πολὺν χρόνον] coni. Ch. (secundum Clitarchus 132):
ἐπὶ πολλῷ χρόνῳ Π Elt.: ἐν πολλῷ χρόνῳ Y.
Sententia a copt. valde libere vertitur: "Someone
who claims to believe, even if he pretends this
for a long time, will not abide but will perish."
326a ἐάν] Π Y: ἂν coni. Elt. Ch. / ἦθος] vertitur
"heart" (ⲍⲏⲧ) copt / ἔσται Y copt lat[JS] etc. sy[1]
Ch.: ἔστω Π rell. lat sy[2] Elt. (sed vide notam eius).
326b ἦθος] sicut 326a copt.
327 βουλευόμενος] coni. Elt. copt latt: βουλόμενος Π
Y (sy[2]?).
330 κάλλιστα οὐσίᾳ] Y latt: καλλίστη οὐσίᾳ copt sy[2]:
τῇ περιουσίᾳ Π.
331 ἀνιάτως ἔχοντα] vertitur "if he is mad" (ⲉϥϣⲁⲛⲗⲁⲅ
[ⲥⲥⲁ], i.e., εἰ λύσσῃ) copt.

323 Fear of death grieves a man inexperienced in soul.

324 It would be best if murderous weapons did not exist, but since they do, do not think they are for you.

325 Especially in matters of faith, no pretense remains hidden for very long.

326a Whatever your character, so also your way of life.

326b A devout character produces a blessed way of life.

327 Whoever devises evil for another is the first to experience evil.

328 Do not let an ungrateful person keep you from doing good.

329 If when asked you are quite willing to give something up, do not deem it of more worth than the person who would receive it.

330 You will use possessions best in sharing them willingly with the needy.

331 Persuade a brother who lacks judgment not to act out of ignorance and keep him safe if he cannot mend his ways.

332 εὐγνωμοσύνῃ πάντας ἀνθρώπους νικᾶν ἀγωνίζου.
333 νοῦν οὐ πρότερον ἕξεις πρὶν ἢ γνῷς οὐκ ἔχων.
334 αὐτάρκειαν ἄσκει.
335 τὰ μέλη τοῦ σώματος τοῖς οὐ χρωμένοις φορτία.
336 ὑπηρετεῖν κρεῖττον ἑτέροις ἢ πρὸς ἄλλων ὑπηρετεῖσθαι.
337 ὃν οὐκ ἀπαλλάττει ὁ θεὸς τοῦ σώματος μὴ βαρυνέσθω.
338 δόγμα ἀκοινώνητον οὐ μόνον ἔχειν ἀλλὰ καὶ ἀκούειν
χαλεπὸν ἡγοῦ.
339 ὁ διδοὺς ὁτιοῦν μετ' ὀνείδους ὑβρίζει.
340 κηδόμενος ὀρφανῶν πατὴρ ἔσῃ πλειόνων τέκνων θεοφιλής.
341 ᾧ ἂν ὑπουργήσῃς ἕνεκα δόξης, μισθοῦ ὑπούργησας.
342 ἐάν τι δῷς ἐπὶ τὸ αὐτὸ γνωσθῆναι, οὐκ ἀνθρώπῳ δέδωκας,
ἰδίᾳ δὲ ἡδονῇ.
343 ὀργὴν πλήθους μὴ παρόξυνε.
344 μάθε τοίνυν τί δεῖ ποιεῖν τὸν εὐδαιμονήσοντα.
345 κρεῖττον ἀποθανεῖν λιμῷ ἢ διὰ γαστρὸς ἀκρασίαν ψυχὴν
ἀμαυρῶσαι.
346 ἐκμαγεῖον τὸ σῶμά σου νόμιζε τῆς ψυχῆς· καθαρὸν οὖν
τήρει.

---

334 = 98.
335 Apud initium add. copt: "There is also this saying"
(ⲡⲓϣⲁϫⲉ ⲟⲛ ⲡⲉ).
338 Ἀκοινώνητον = "not sharing in community." It can
therefore refer to a failure to share goods, etc.,
with others (so copt, latt - cf. Sextus 296) but
also to the holding of views not shared by the
community.
339 ὑβρίζει] Add. καὶ εἰς θεὸν ἁμαρτάνει Y (copt?).
341 Om. Y / ᾧ] Π (copt?): ὃ latt sy². Cf. Mt. 6.1-4.
342 υm. Y / τι δῷς] coni. Elt. latt sy¹: δίδως Π (copt?).
344 εὐδαιμονήσοντα] coni. Elt. latt sy¹: εὐδαιμονήσαντα
Y čopt: ευγνωμονοῦντα Π sy².
346 ἐκμαγεῖον] Π Y: ἱμάτιον copt latt sy² / καθαρὸν . . .
τήρει] add. καθὼς ἀναμάρτητον copt sy².

332 Strive to surpass everyone in good judgment.

333 You will not have understanding until you know that you do not have it.

334 Practice self-sufficiency.

335 Bodily members are burdensome to those who do not make use of them.

336 It is better to serve other people than to be served by anyone.

337 The person whom God does not release from the body should not be upset.

338 Consider it dangerous not only to hold a novel teaching but even to listen to it.

339 Whoever combines gift-giving with reproach acts insultingly.

340 Whoever cares for orphans will be a father of many children and loved by God.

341 Whomever you serve for glory, you have served for pay.

342 If you give something in order to attract attention, you have not given it for the sake of humanity but for your own pleasure.

343 Do not stir up the anger of the multitude.

344 Learn, therefore, what the person who would be happy must do.

345 It is better to die of hunger than to impair the soul through gluttony.

346 Consider that your body bears the imprint of the soul. Therefore keep it pure.

58

347 ὁποῖα ἂν ἐπιτηδεύσῃ ψυχὴ ἐνοικοῦσα τῷ σώματι,
    τοιαῦτα μαρτύρια ἔχουσα ἄπεισιν ἐπὶ τὴν κρίσιν.
348 ἀκαθάρτου ψυχῆς ἀκάθαρτοι δαίμονες ἀντιποιοῦνται.
349 πιστὴν ψυχὴν καὶ ἀγαθὴν ἐν ὁδῷ θεοῦ κακοὶ δαίμονες
    οὐκ ἐμποδίζουσιν.
350 λόγου περὶ θεοῦ μὴ παντὶ κοινώνει.
351 οὐκ ἀσφαλὲς ἀκούειν περὶ θεοῦ τοῖς ὑπὸ δόξης διεφθαρ-
    μένοις.
352 περὶ θεοῦ καὶ τἀληθῆ λέγειν κίνδυνος οὐ μικρός.

353 περὶ θεοῦ μηδὲν εἴπῃς μὴ μαθὼν παρὰ θεοῦ.
354 ἀθέῳ περὶ θεοῦ μηδὲν εἴπῃς.
355 περὶ θεοῦ λόγον ἀληθῆ ὡς θεὸν τίμα.
356 μὴ καθαρεύων ἀνοσίων ἔργων μὴ ϕθέγξῃ περὶ θεοῦ λόγον.

357 λόγος ἀληθὴς περὶ θεοῦ λόγος ἐστὶν θεοῦ.
358 πεισθεὶς πρότερον θεοφιλὴς εἶναι πρὸς οὓς ἂν πεισθῇς
    λέγε περὶ θεοῦ.

---

347 ὁποῖα] Y copt latt sy²: ὁποῖα δ' Π Elt. Ch.
349 οὐκ ἐμποδίζουσιν] vertitur "they will not be able to
    restrain" (ⲚⲀⲱϤⲕⲀⲧⲉⲭⲉ... ⲉⲚ [from Gk. κατέχω]) copt.
350 λόγου] coni. Elt.: λόγῳ Π Y.
352 τἀληθῆ] Π latt Orig. (*In Ezech.* 1.11): τἀληθὲς Y:
    τὴν ἀλήθειαν copt (sic videtur sed fortasse versio
    aliquantum libera habetur).
354 ἀθέῳ] Π copt lat^AVS: ἀθέῳ δὲ Y (rell. lat.?) Elt. Ch.
355 Post 356 sy², post 357 copt / ἀληθῆ] Π Y latt sy²:
    λέγε copt / ὡς θεὸν] Π latt: ὡς θεοῦ Y sy²:
    ὡς παρὰ θεῷ copt / τίμα] om. copt.
358 πεισθῇς] Π: πεῖσαι θέλῃς coni. Lloyd-Jones copt /
    add. τότε ante λέγε copt latt sy¹.

347 Whatever a soul pursues while inhabiting the
body will accompany it as evidence when it goes
to judgment.

348 Unclean demons lay claim to an unclean soul.

349 Evil demons do not prevent a faithful and good soul
from following God's way.

350 Do not talk about God with everyone.

351 It is not safe for those corrupted by fame to
hear about God.

352 To speak even the truth about God involves no
small risk.

353 Say nothing about God which you have not learned
from God.

354 Say nothing about God to the godless.

355 Honor a true word about God as you would honor
God Himself.

356 If you are not cleansed of unholy deeds, do not
utter a word about God.

357 The true word about God is God's word.

358 When you are persuaded that you love God, then
speak about God to those whom you would persuade.

60

359 τὰ ἔργα σου θεοφιλῆ προηγείσθω παντὸς λόγου περὶ
θεοῦ.

360 ἐπὶ πλήθους λέγειν περὶ θεοῦ μὴ ἐπιτήδευε.

361 λόγου περὶ θεοῦ φείδου μᾶλλον ἢ περὶ ψυχῆς.

362 ψυχὴν αἱρετώτερον ἢ λόγον εἰκῆ προέσθαι περὶ θεοῦ.

363a θεοφιλοῦς ἀνδρὸς σώματος μὲν ἄρξεις, λόγου δὲ οὐ
κυριεύσεις.

363b σοφοῦ σώματος καὶ λέων ἄρχει, τούτου δὴ μόνου καὶ
τύραννος.

364 ὑπὸ τυράννου γινομένης ἀπειλῆς τίνος εἶ τότε μάλιστα
μέμνησο.

365 λόγον οἷς οὐ θέμις ὁ λέγων περὶ θεοῦ προδότης θεοῦ
νομιζέσθω.

366 λόγον περὶ θεοῦ σιγᾶν ἄμεινον ἢ προπετῶς διαλέγεσθαι.

367 ὁ λέγων ψευδῆ περὶ θεοῦ καταψεύδεται θεοῦ.

368 ἄνθρωπος μηδὲν ἔχων λέγειν περὶ θεοῦ ἀληθὲς ἔρημός
ἐστιν θεοῦ.

369 θεὸν οὐκ ἔστιν γινώσκειν μὴ σεβόμενον.

370 οὐκ ἔστιν ὅπως ἀδικῶν τις ἄνθρωπον σέβοι τὸν θεόν.

371 κρηπὶς θεοσεβείας φιλανθρωπία.

372 ὁ προνοῶν ἀνθρώπων εὐχόμενός τε ὑπὲρ πάντων οὗτος
ἀληθείᾳ θεοῦ νομιζέσθω.

373 θεοῦ μὲν ἴδιον τὸ σώζειν οὓς ἂν προαιρῆται.

---

361 ἢ περὶ ψυχῆς] Π Υ copt latt Elt.: ἢ ψυχῆς coni. Ch.
370 Om. Π.
371 κρηπὶς] Π Υ: κρηπὶς καὶ ἀρχὴ latt: ἀρχὴ copt sy[2].
372 νομιζέσθω] om. copt.

359 Let your works of divine love precede every word about God.

360 Do not make it your business to speak to the multitude about God.

361 Talk less about God than about the soul.

362 It is better to squander a soul than a word about God.

363a You may have power over the body of a man who loves God but you will not control his reason.

363b As a lion has power over the body of a sage so like-wise does a tyrant--but only over his body.

364 When a tyrant threatens, then especially remember to Whom you belong.

365 Consider anyone a betrayer of God who speaks a word about God to those who have no right to hear.

366 In talk about God, silence is better than reckless words.

367 The person who utters falsehoods about God slanders Him.

368 A person who has nothing true to say about God is abandoned by Him.

369 A person who does not worship God cannot know Him.

370 It is not possible for anyone who wrongs a human being to worship God.

371 Love of humanity is the foundation stone of divine worship.

372 Whoever is considerate of all human beings and prays for them should be considered as truly of God.

373 It is proper to God to save those whom He chooses.

62

374 εὐσεβοῦς δὲ τὸ εὔχεσθαι θεῷ σώζειν.
375 ὁπόταν εὐξαμένῳ σοι γένηται ὑπὸ τοῦ θεοῦ, τότε
ἐξουσίαν ἔχειν ἡγοῦ παρὰ θεῷ.
376a ἄξιος ἄνθρωπος θεοῦ θεὸς ἐν ἀνθρώποις.
376b θεὸς καὶ υἱὸς θεοῦ τὸ μὲν ἄριστον, τὸ δὲ ἐγγυτάτω
τοῦ ἀρίστου.
377 ἀκτήμονα κρεῖττον ἢ ἀκοινώνητον εἶναι πολυκτήμονα.
378 μὴ διδοὺς δεομένοις δυνατὸς ὢν οὐ λήψῃ δεόμενος
παρὰ θεοῦ.
379 τροφῆς δεομένῳ μεταδιδόντος ἐξ ὅλης ψυχῆς δόμα μέν
τι βραχύ, προθυμία δὲ μεγάλη παρὰ θεῷ.

---

374 σώζειν] Π Υ: σώζειν πάντας (ἀνθρώπους) copt latt
sy².
376a Add. ad finem (ab initio 376b) καὶ υἱὸς θεοῦ copt.
376b Om. latt. θεὸς . . . θεοῦ] om. copt (itaque "The
Great One exists as does he who is next to the Great
One"). "For God and the Son of God are on an
equality with the Holy Spirit" sy².
377 ἀκοινώνητον] om. copt. / add. ad finem (ab initio 378)
μὴ διδοὺς δεομένοις copt.
378 μὴ . . . ὢν] om. copt -- id quod relictum coniungitur
cum 377 (itaque "But as for you [when you act in that
way], if you entreat God, He will not give to you.").
379 ὅλης] Υ copt: om. Π latt sy² / δεομένῳ] Π Υ latt:
δεομένοις copt sy² / μεγάλη] hic sequuntur 488-89
Π. Cf. Mk. 12.30 = Dt. 6.5 LXX.

374 But it is proper to the religious person to pray to God to give salvation.

375 Whenever your prayer is granted by God, then consider that you have power from God.

376a A human being worthy of God is a god among human beings.

376b If God is best, then a son of God is next best.

377 It is better to have nothing than to have many things and share them with no one.

378 If when you can you do not give to the needy, you will not receive from God when you are in need.

379 When someone shares food readily with a needy person, his gift is something small but his readiness to share is in God's sight something great indeed.

64

380 θεὸν οὐ νομίζοντος ὁ νομίζων καὶ οὐδὲν εἶναι πρὸς
αὑτὸν ἡγούμενος οὐχ ἧττον ἄθεος.

381 τιμᾷ θεὸν ἄριστα ὁ τὴν ἑαυτοῦ διάνοιαν ἐξομοιώσας
θεῷ εἰς δύναμιν.

382 θεὸς δεῖται μὲν οὐδαμῇ οὐδενός, χαίρει δὲ τοῖς
μεταδιδοῦσι τοῖς δεομένοις.

383 πιστῶν ὀλίγοι μὲν ἔστωσαν οἱ λόγοι, ἔργα δὲ πολλά.

384 πιστὸς φιλομαθὴς ἐργάτης ἀληθείας.

385 ἁρμόζου πρὸς τὰς περιστάσεις ἵνα εὐθυμῇς.

386 μηδένα ἀδικῶν οὐδένα φοβηθήσῃ.

387 τύραννος εὐδαιμονίαν οὐκ ἀφαιρεῖται.

388 ὃ δεῖ ποιεῖν, ἑκὼν ποίει.

389a ὃ μὴ δεῖ ποιεῖν, μηδενὶ τρόπῳ ποίει.

389b πάντα μᾶλλον ἢ τὸ σοφὸς εἶναι ὑπισχνοῦ.

390 οὗ καλῶς πράττεις τὴν αἰτίαν ἀνάφερε εἰς θεόν.

391 οὐδεὶς σοφὸς ἀνὴρ κάτω που βλέπων εἰς γῆν καὶ
τραπέζας.

392 τὸν φιλόσοφον οὐ τὸν χρηματισμὸν ἐλευθεροῦν δεῖ,
ἀλλὰ τὴν ψυχήν.

393 ψεύδεσθαι φυλάττου· ἔστιν γὰρ ἀπατᾶν καὶ ἀπατᾶσθαι.

394 τίς θεὸς γνῶθι· γνῶθι δὲ τί τὸ νοοῦν ἐν σοί.

395 θεοῦ καλὸν ἔργον ἀγαθὸς ἄνθρωπος.

396 ἄθλιοι δι' οὓς ὁ λόγος ἀκούει κακῶς.

397 ψυχὴν θάνατος οὐκ ἀπόλλυσιν ἀλλὰ κακὸς βίος.

---

380 ὁ νομίζων οὐδὲν εἶναι πρὸς θεὸν οὐχ ἧττων θεοῦ
copt (sic videtur) / ἧττον ἄθεος] coni. Lloyd-Jones
(latt?): ἥττονα θεός Π: ἧττον ἢ ἄθεος Υ.
381 Post 385 Υ.
382 οὐδαμη] Π Υ latt: om. copt sy².
387 εὐδαιμονίαν] vertitur "the kingdom" (ⲦⲘⲚⲦⲢ̄[ⲣⲟ]) copt.
388 Om. Υ.
392 ἐλευθεροῦν] Π (ἐλευθεροῖν) Υ: ἐλεύθερον εἶναι latt:
εὐλογεῖν copt (sy²?).
393 γάρ] Π Υ (sy²?): om. copt latt.
394 γνῶθι δὲ τί] copt: καὶ τί latt: τί τὸ ν. ἔστιν ἐν
σ. Π: μάθε Υ sy². [Haplography caused the omission of
the second γνῶθι and various efforts were then made
to repair the text.]
397 Hic desinit copt.

380 Whoever believes in a God who is not concerned about anything is just as godless as an unbeliever.

381 He honors God best who conforms his mind to God as far as possible.

382 God needs nothing at all, but He rejoices in those who share with the needy.

383 Let the words of believers be few but their deeds many.

384 A believer who is fond of learning is a doer of truth.

385 Adjust to circumstances in order to be happy.

386 If you harm no one you will fear no one.

387 No tyrant takes away happiness.

388 Do willingly what you must do.

389a Do not ever do what you must not do.

389b Claim anything except that you are wise.

390 Give God the credit for whatever you do well.

391 No wise man looks down upon the earth or upon tables.

392 The philosopher must be free not in name but in reality.

393 Beware of lying, for to deceive is to be deceived.

394 Know who God is; know the understanding that is within you.

395 A good person is a noble work of God.

396 Wretched are those who give the word an evil reputation.

397 Not death but an evil life destroys the soul.

398 πρὸς ὃ γέγονας εἰδὼς γνώσῃ σαυτόν.
399 οὐκ ἔστιν κατὰ θεὸν ζῆν ἄνευ τοῦ σωφρόνως καὶ καλῶς
καὶ δικαίως πράττειν.
400 ἀνθρώπων ἀπίστων βίος ὄνειδος.
401 μήποτε λάθῃς σαυτὸν ἀγενεῖ φύσει μεταδιδοὺς λόγου
θεοῦ.
402 ψυχὴν ἀπὸ γῆς πίστις ἀνάγει παρὰ θεόν.
403 σοφοῦ ψυχῆς μέγεθος οὐκ ἂν ἐξεύροις μᾶλλον ἤπερ καὶ
θεοῦ.
404 ὅσα δίδωσιν ὁ θεὸς οὐδεὶς ἀφαιρεῖται.
405 ὃ παρέχει κόσμος βεβαίως οὐ τηρεῖ.
406 θεία σοφία ἡ τοῦ θεοῦ γνῶσις.
407 ἀκαθάρτῳ ψυχῇ μὴ τόλμα λέγειν περὶ θεοῦ.
408 ἀνδρὸς πεῖραν πρότερον ἔργων ἢ λόγων ποίει.
409 τὰ ὦτά σου μὴ παντὶ πίστευε.
410 οἴεσθαι μὲν περὶ θεοῦ εὐμαρές, λέγειν δὲ ἀληθὲς
μόνῳ τῷ δικαίῳ συγκεχώρηται.
411 μὴ βασανίσῃς σου τῇ ψυχῇ τὸ σῶμα μηδὲ τὴν ψυχήν
σου βασανίσῃς ταῖς τοῦ σώματος ἡδοναῖς.
412 ἔθιζε σεαυτὸν τῷ μὲν σώματι παρέχειν τὰ τοῦ
σώματος σωφρόνως, τῇ δὲ ψυχῇ θεοσεβῶς.
413 τρέφε σου τὴν μὲν ψυχὴν λόγῳ θείῳ, τὸ δὲ σῶμα σιτίοις
λιτοῖς.
414 χαίρειν ἔθιζέ σου τὴν ψυχὴν ἐφ᾽ οἷς καλὸν χαίρειν.

---

398 Om. Π.
399 ἄνευ . . . δικαίως] coni. Elt (secundum Clitarchus
123) pl. lat (sy[1]?): om. καὶ καλῶς Π lat[OS]: καὶ
δικαίως ἄνευ τοῦ σωφρόνος sy[2]: δικαίως καὶ
σωφρόνος Υ.
404 = 92 (ἃ).
405 Om. lat[SÜ] syy. Post 405 sequuntur 236-61 Π.
407 = 451 (ἀκολάστῳ).
410 Om. Υ.
412 Om. Υ.
414 Om. Υ sy[2].

398 When you know for what reason you exist, you
will know yourself.
399 It is not possible to live in accord with God without
acting moderately, graciously and righteously.
400 The life of those without faith is a disgrace.
401 Never, even unwittingly, should you share the word
of God with those of a vile nature.
402 Faith guides the soul from earth to God.
403 You will not discover the greatness of a sage's
soul any more than the greatness of God.
404 Whatever God gives, no one takes away.
405 What the world offers, it does not keep secure.
406 The knowledge of God is divine wisdom.
407 Do not dare to speak about God to an impure soul.
408 Test a man's works before his words.
409 Do not believe everything you hear.
410 To offer suppositions about God is easy, but to
speak the truth is possible only for the righteous
man.
411 Do not torture your body with your soul nor your
soul with the pleasures of the body.
412 Accustom yourself to provide for the needs of the
body with moderation and for the needs of the
soul with devotion.
413 Nourish your soul with the divine word but your body
with plain food.
414 Accustom your soul to rejoice in whatever it
should rejoice.

68

415a ψυχὴ χαίρουσα ἐπὶ μικροῖς ἄτιμος παρὰ θεῷ.
415b σοφοῦ ψυχὴ ἀκούει θεοῦ.
416 σοφοῦ ψυχὴ ἁρμόζεται πρὸς θεὸν ὑπὸ θεοῦ.
417 σοφοῦ ψυχὴ ἀεὶ θεὸν ὁρᾷ.
418 ψυχὴ σοφοῦ σύνεστιν ἀεὶ θεῷ.
419 καρδία θεοφιλοῦς ἐν χειρὶ θεοῦ ἵδρυται.
420 ψυχῆς ἄνοδος πρὸς θεὸν διὰ λόγου θεοῦ.
421 σοφὸς ἕπεται θεῷ καὶ ὁ θεὸς ψυχῇ σοφοῦ.
422 χαίρει τῷ ἀρχομένῳ τὸ ἄρχον, καὶ ὁ θεὸς οὖν
     σοφῷ χαίρει.
423 ἀχώριστόν ἐστιν τοῦ ἀρχομένου τὸ ἄρχον, καὶ θεὸς
     οὖν τοῦ σοφοῦ προνοεῖ καὶ κήδεται.
424 ἐπιτροπεύεται σοφὸς ἀνὴρ ὑπὸ θεοῦ, διὰ τοῦτο καὶ
     μακάριος.
425 ψυχὴ σοφοῦ δοκιμάζεται διὰ σώματος ὑπὸ θεοῦ.
426 οὐχ ἡ γλῶττα τοῦ σοφοῦ τιμία παρὰ θεῷ, ἀλλ' ἡ
     φρόνησις.
427 σοφὸς ἀνὴρ καὶ σιγῶν τὸν θεὸν τιμᾷ [εἰδὼς διὰ τίνα
     σιγᾷ].
428 γαστρὸς καὶ τῶν ὑπὸ γαστέρα ὁ μὴ κρατῶν οὐδεὶς
     πιστός.

429 ἄνθρωπος ἀκρατὴς μιαίνει τὸν θεόν.
430 ἄνθρωπον θεοῦ γνῶσις βραχύλογον ποιεῖ.
431 πολλοὺς λόγους περὶ θεοῦ ἀπειρία ποιεῖ.
432 θεὸν ἄνθρωπος εἰδὼς οὐ πολλὰ κομπάζει.
433 ἐκλεκτὸς ἄνθρωπος ποιεῖ μὲν πάντα κατὰ θεόν, εἶναι
     δὲ οὐχ ὑπισχνεῖται.

415a Om. Y.
416   Om. Y.
419   Cf. Wis. 3.1.
421   Add. ad finem (ab initio 422) χαίρει Y sy².
423   ἐστιν] Π pl. lat: ἀεὶ Y.
427   Om. Y / εἰδὼς . . . σιγᾷ] Π: om. latt syy (cf.
      Sextus 589). Post 427 sequuntur 455-88 Π.
428   Om. Y.
430   θεοῦ] Π latt sy²: om. Y.
431-43   Om. Π.

415a A soul which rejoices over trivial matters is dishonored before God.

415b The soul of the sage hearkens to God.

416 Through God the soul of the sage is attuned to God.

417 The soul of the sage always perceives God.

418 The soul of the sage is always in union with God.

419 The heart of one who loves God is secure in the hand of God.

420 Through God's word the soul ascends to God.

421 The sage accompanies God and God accompanies the soul of the sage.

422 Anything that rules takes pleasure in what it rules, and so God takes pleasure in the sage.

423 Anything that rules is inseparable from what it rules, and so God watches over and cares for the sage.

424 The wise man is governed by God and so is blessed.

425 Through the body the sage's soul is tested by God.

426 It is not the sage's tongue that is valued by God, but his prudence.

427 Even while silent the wise man honors God [since he knows on Whose behalf he is silent].

428 No one is faithful who does not control his stomach and his lower organs.

429 The person who lacks self-control defiles God.

430 Knowledge of God produces a man of few words.

431 A lack of experience leads to excessive talk about God.

432 A person who knows God does not boast a great deal.

433 One who is chosen does all things in accord with God but he does not claim to be chosen.

70

434 *
435 ἄνθρωπος δὶς ἐμπιπλώμενος τροφῇ καὶ μηδέποτε μόνος
κοιμώμενος νύκτωρ συνουσίας οὐ φεύγει.
436a εἱμαρμένη πιστὸν οὐ ποιεῖ.
436b εἱμαρμένη θεοῦ χάριτος οὐκ ἄρχει· εἰ δὲ μή, καὶ θεοῦ.
437 *
438 πιστὸς ἀνὴρ τρέφεται ἐγκρατείᾳ.
439 γνῶθι ῥήματα καὶ κτίσματα θεοῦ καὶ τίμα κατ᾽ ἀξίαν
τὸν θεόν.
440 *
441 ψυχὴ πιστὴ ἀγνὴ καὶ σοφὴ καὶ προφῆτις ἀληθείας θεοῦ.
442 οὐκ ἀγαπήσεις τὸν θεὸν οὐκ ἔχων ἐν ἑαυτῷ οἷον
ὁ θεός.
443 φίλον ἡγοῦ τὸ ὅμοιον τῷ ὁμοίῳ.
444 οὐκ ἀγαπῶν τὸν θεὸν οὐκ ἔσῃ παρὰ θεῷ.
445 ἔθιζε σεαυτὸν ἀεὶ ἀφορᾶν πρὸς τὸν θεόν.
446 ὁρῶν τὸν θεὸν ὄψῃ σεαυτόν.
447 ὁρῶν τὸν θεὸν ποιήσεις τὸ ἐν σοὶ φρονοῦν ὁποῖον ὁ
θεός.
448 σέβου τὸ ἐν σοὶ καὶ ταῖς τοῦ σώματος ἐπιθυμίαις
μὴ καθυβρίσῃς.
449 ἀσπίλωτόν σου τὸ σῶμα τήρει ὡς ἔνδυμα τῆς ψυχῆς
παρὰ θεοῦ, ὡς καὶ τὸν χιτῶνά σου τηρεῖς ἀσπίλωτον
ἔνδυμα ὄντα τῆς σαρκός.
450 σοφοῦ διάνοια θεοῦ ἔνοπτρον.
451 ἀκολάστῳ ψυχῇ μὴ τόλμα λέγειν περὶ θεοῦ.

434 Om. etiam Y: *Fidelis homo semper in metu est,
usquequo eat ad Deum* latt.
437 Om. etiam Y: *Graviter accipit libidines corporis
vir fidelis* latt.
439 τίμα . . . θεόν] Y: τίμα ἕκαστον κατ᾽ ἀξίαν μετὰ
θεόν latt sy².
440 Om. etiam Y: *Nihil proprium Dei ducas quod malum est*
latt.
442 τὸν θεόν] lat^GU (cf. Gild.) sy²: κύριον τὸν θεὸν Y
pl. lat Elt. Ch. (cf. Mt. 22.37 / Mk. 12.30 / Lk.
10.27 = Dt. 6.5 LXX) / θεός] latt sy²: θεὸς θέλει Y.
443 Found twice in Aristotle (*Eth. Nic.* 8.1155a34 and
9.1165b17).
446 Om. Y.
448 Om. Y.
451 = 407 (ἀκαθάρτῳ). Om. Π syy.

434   A believer is always anxious until he attains
      to God.

435   A person who eats a double portion and never sleeps
      alone at night does not avoid becoming like his
      passions.

436a Fate does not produce a believer.

436b Fate does not control God's grace or else it would
      control God as well.

437   A faithful man provides a poor welcome for
      bodily lusts.

438   A faithful man is nurtured in self-control.

439   Know the words and works of God and honor God
      accordingly.

440   Consider nothing that is evil as belonging to God.

441   A faithful soul is pure and wise, a prophet of
      God's truth.

442   You will not love God if you do not have that which
      is of God within yourself.

443   Know that like is dear to like.

444   If you do not love God you will not be in God's
      presence.

445   Accustom yourself to look only toward God.

446   If you perceive God you will perceive yourself.

447   If you perceive God you will conform your mind
      to God.

448   Reverence what is within you and do not insult
      it with bodily lusts.

449   Keep spotless your body, the garment of the soul
      given by God, just as you keep spotless your coat,
      the garment of the flesh.

450   The mind of the sage is a mirror of God.

451   Do not dare to speak about God to an undisciplined
      soul.